I0107440

TO HELP PUSH

AND

PULL ME THROUGH

AN AMAZING STORY INSPIRED BY TRUE EVENTS

Spencer Lennard Smith

Copyright © 2015 by Spencer Lennard Smith
Los Angeles, California
All rights reserved
Printed and Bound in the United States of America

Published by
Spencer's Publishing
Los Angeles, California
E-mail: smith-spencer@hotmail.com

Packaging/Consulting
Professional Publishing House
1425 W. Manchester Ave. Ste. B
Los Angeles, California 90047
323-750-3592
E-mail: professionalpublishinghouse@yahoo.com
www.Professionalpublishinghouse.com

Cover design: Jay De Vance, III
Illustration: Jay De Vance, III
First printing April 2016
978-0-69268229-6
10987654321

No part of this book may be reproduced, stored in a retrieval system, or transmitted in any form or by any means without the prior
written permission of the publisher—except by a reviewer who
may quote brief passages in a review to be printed in a newspaper,
magazine, or journal.

For inquiries, contact: smith-spencer@hotmail.com

Dedications

God bless the hands that helped me with creating this story

Irene B. Jones

And

Robert L. Smith

ACKNOWLEDGMENTS

I want to acknowledge the many families in the inner cities that are looking for a way to Help and Pull Others Through. May God bless you all with the perseverance and resilience that is needed to get through life.

JUST TO NAME A FEW...

Adam	Garcia	Morris
Allum	Galloway	Myers
Armstead	Gray	Paige
Atkins	Griffith	Phillip
Berry	Gonzales	Philpot
Blair	Gilliam	Potts
Bradford	Harris	Perez
Brown	Hawthorne	Reynolds
Brim	Hill	Smith
Calloway	Jackson	Tatum
Crane	Jenkins	Tucker
Carpenter	Johnson	Turner
Chandler	Jones	Ware
Chisolm	Lee	Whites
Coles	Lemon	Whitfield
Danford	Maxwell	Williams
Fishers	Miles	Wise

My Prayer

O God, please give me the strength to endure what I must in order to achieve what I need to succeed.

CHAPTER 1

I was conceived in the midst of two raging wars at the early part of 1965. One war was in my country where my people were battling for equal liberties, equal rights, and equal opportunities. And the other war was right in the home of my parents.

My mother and father, from my understanding, loved each other dearly. My father was a young, proud, father-to-be, and the living seemed pretty easy . . . as long as he stayed in his place in society.

A pivotal point arose for my father when the workforce began to deny many of the black men employment. Later that same year, in August, a riot broke out in the Watts section of Los Angeles.

My father struggled daily pretending to be the man he desired to be. But, without steady employment, he felt he couldn't be a man. His light was burning dim, and it also brought strife and humiliation into the household. Some people would call it the blues. But it was nothing compared to the pain of childbirth my mother endured when I was born October 14, 1965, in the city of Compton, California, in the backseat of my daddy's green and white 1959 Buick Electra. They were parked in the driveway of our sky-blue miniature-sized home on Orr Avenue with no one around to help; it was just my mother, my father, and God, pushing and pulling me through. And it's been that way ever since. My parents named me Nathaniel. That day, October 14, 1965, was actually the beginning of the end of my nuclear family. For many reasons, for the first five years after the day I was born, my parents' relationship was rocky. My mother, Bernice Jones, wanted to go right, and my father, Cornelius Smith, wanted to go left. Therefore, a split ensued; however, my parents weren't married, so a divorce wasn't necessary. Yes, that meant I was born out of wedlock. My mother subsequently took her baby boy and moved to Watts, California, on the opposite side of the affluent part of the city, with the help of the Aid To Needy Children Program, in a small house on Hickory Street.

I can vividly remember our house. It seemed to be a little bigger than the house in Compton, where I had shared a bedroom with my parents. This house was a small, two-bedroom, avocado-green house with dingy-white trimming around the windowpane and wall-to-wall dark-brown shag carpet throughout. The floors creaked when we walked around.

I had my own bedroom where my mother painted the walls blue and gold because we were both Los Angeles Rams fans. I had a set of bunk beds with Speed Racer printed quilts. I kept a large jelly jar of marbles on my closet shelf. I also had a two-level bookshelf where I kept all the exciting books I loved to read like *The Wizard of Oz, Rumpelstiltskin*, and *The Three Little Pigs.* On my seventh birthday, my mother bought me a 13-inch black-and-white television, but I could only watch it on the weekends. I would watch Channel 52 with *The Three Stooges, Giant Robot*, and *Speed Racer.* I'd watch that channel all night until the programming went off, fading into black-and-white fuzzy, squiggly lines.

My mother's room was just a little larger than mine with bright-green paint on the walls. She kept a variety of perfumes on her dresser. She also had over a dozen dresses hung up around her room as her closet was tightly filled to capacity with more clothing.

In our overcrowded kitchen with walls decorated in red and green flower wallpaper and black-and-white checkered linoleum flooring is where I could always find my mother cooking up a meal. The kitchen was the place where I really started to pay more attention to my mother. She was a stern, proud, petite lady with a round face and high cheekbones, and she wore her hair pulled back in an Afro puff. She had pretty brown eyes, her skin was like dark chocolate, and she weighed about 107 pounds. When she would cook in the heat, she'd sometimes have a stream of sweat running down the side of her face; her skin looked like melting hot chocolate. The kitchen was where she honed her cooking skills and spent an enormous amount of time making homemade ice cream,

German chocolate and coconut layer cakes, and apple and lemon meringue pies.

I loved it when she made her peach cobbler. My job was to help her take the skins off the peaches. After being dropped in boiling hot water, and then plunged into ice-cold water, the skins then came off easily. The sticky peach juice got all over my hands and slowly worked its way down my arms until I was a sticky mess. My mother never got mad at me about how messy my clothes would become. She would simply laugh and smile with a sympathetic expression that said, "you poor thing." The smell of peaches filled the air.

My mother reveled in colorful cooking, using lots of spices and various cooking methods. Whenever she made her collard greens, she'd place them in a large pot of water with vinegar and ham hocks, while mixing in chicken broth. She'd then season with salt and pepper, bringing them to a boil, and reducing the heat to a low simmer for an hour.

The aroma would evoke a strong emotional response from the neighbors. They would come knocking on our door for the obvious reason: to come get a plate of those collard greens. My mother's collard greens were the best; however, I loved it when she would spoil me with ice cream—any flavor would do. We had a small dining room with a breakfront and a wooden dining-room table with matching rickety chairs. Momma covered the table with a flowered tablecloth and place mats; she placed cushions on all the chairs.

CHAPTER 2

h

My mother was extremely protective of me. She would gently remind me that I was her first priority as she struggled daily to provide a modest lifestyle for both of us. As she began working for the Watts Labor Community Action Committee (WLCAC) as a secretary, she would often bring her work home. WLCAC was started in Watts after the riots, and its goal was to apply union skills and organizational experience to improve and revitalize the Watts community. Their slogan was "Don't Move . . . Improve." She was there when the city's mayoral race had come to an end, ushering out its old mayor, Sam Yorty, and delivering the city's first black mayor, Tom Bradley. The city was on the upswing.

My mother had this little Remington typewriter. Most of the time when she wasn't at work or cooking, she would prop herself up in one of our rickety chairs at that old wooden brown table, and then she would start pecking away on that typewriter until I'd hear the little bell sound at the end of all the pecking. Then the clickety-clack and pecking would resume.

My mother was what some people would call a chain-smoker, and her cigarette of choice was Benson & Hedges menthol. As the room filled with smoke, so did the ashtray next to her typewriter with the cigarette butts. As she lit a cigarette and deeply inhaled, she'd put it down long enough to type a chain of letters as a part of her job just before the next little bell sounded. She'd be pecking and smoking sometimes all throughout the night in that smoke-filled room.

She also enjoyed entertaining friends and family from time to time by giving parties and hosting gatherings in our very small living room. Our guests would manage to squeeze in, and they would seem to be having so much fun sitting around on our red and black crushed velvet, plastic-covered couch with matching love seat. I would sometimes stop in while headed to my room from the kitchen and watch everything going on and pay attention to everyone speaking until my mother would yell at me to get out of grown people's business and get in my room. She would let me come into the gatherings when some of the guests would pay me money to emulate the latest singers and dancers like Jackie Wilson and James Brown. I used to mimic the singers in the middle of the floor with a broomstick as a microphone, singing and doing the splits. It was a lot of fun. The ladies would grab me and shower me with kisses all over my face. I guess I was like their only little entertainer at the time.

My mother had a lot of self-respect, which gave me no reason to disrespect her. She had a very well-honed sense of humor, and sometimes she would incorporate a few curse words in her jokes. The first time I heard my mother curse was when she was entertaining a room full of guests at one of her small boxing match parties, when Ali and Frazier had their first fight on TV. Ali portrayed Frazier as a "dumb tool of the white establishment." Ali also claimed that Frazier was "too ugly to be champ." Then Ali said, "I'm fighting for the little man in the ghetto." When she went to use the restroom, she noticed the toilet bowl was leaking from the bottom at the base, so she went into the living room and made an announcement to her guests. She said, "Looka here! When you go to use the bathroom, there will be no more leaning over to the side to wipe your ass, because when you rock and lean to the side, you are knocking my toilet off its foundation and it's causing my toilet to leak! Now you have to stand up to wipe your big ass!" The entire room would burst into appreciative laughter, and my mother was tickled pink.

I really liked living on Hickory Street, although it wasn't your average tree-lined street with palm trees and cookie-cutter homes. Many of our streets in Watts had a mix of old and rebuilt homes interspersed with vacant lots. Our cozy little house had a small front yard with patches of grass surrounded by dirt, and in that dirt was where my mother would sometimes find me and my friends on our knees shooting marbles. I had no clue about why Momma always had to yell at me to take a bath at night before going to bed; she had to stay on top of me about my hygiene as a young boy. Bathing was one of my daily chores.

When I was about ten years old, I can remember waking up crying and screaming, thinking I was maybe having a nightmare about the wolf in *The Three Little Pigs* storybook I used to read. When my jar of marbles fell off the closet shelf and the house shook like the big bad wolf was tearing my house down, my mother came running into my room to shelter me in the doorway of my bedroom while trying to explain what an earthquake was, as the shaking slowly began to stop.

Although I enjoyed my house and having my own room, I also missed the comfort and the presence of my father. So I had mixed emotions running all through me when we first moved to Watts. I once overheard my mother having a discussion with one of our neighbors. That is when I heard her say that my father had gone off and married a Caucasian woman by the name of Abigail.

Although my father did not show full support to Momma at the start of my life, she was not so scornful to the extent of denying him the opportunity to play a meaningful part of my life. Therefore, even though my father walked out of our lives, my momma felt that a mother and father raising a child together formed the core structure of the community. And when the community's infrastructure breaks down, then the enemy can invade, resulting in collateral damage to the child as the ills of the community were always lurking about, waiting for an opportune moment to invade.

She also felt that it was important for me to have strong black men as role models.

Speaking of my father, the first time I'd seen him in many years was when I was about eleven years old. I saw my resemblance to him as he looked like an older version of me. He was a slim man who stood about 5 foot 9 and weighed about 165 pounds. He had cocoa-brown skin, brown eyes, wore a pencil-thin mustache, and had a short salt-and-pepper Afro. He worked for the city of Los Angeles as a city maintenance worker. He drove a street sweeper, cleaning many of the streets, wearing a dark green uniform with the city of Los Angeles logo embroidered on the shirt pocket.

He came by one Friday to pick me up to visit him and Abigail for the weekend. My mother was a bit reluctant to let me go spend the weekend with my father; however, she eventually gave in and allowed me to go. He lived on the West side of town in the city of Inglewood near the Inglewood Forum and the Hollywood Racetrack on Ninety-Seventh Street and Prairie Avenue, a tree-lined street with well-manicured yards. His house was a modern two-bedroom gray and black stucco home. It seemed a little more affluent than Watts.

Abigail had baby-blue eyes with a Coppertone suntan. She was a dishwater blonde who stood about 5 foot 2 and weighed about 105 pounds. I guess I would say that my stepmother had an effervescent personality. I couldn't get used to calling her momma as my father suggested that I do. I don't know if it was because she was white, or if it was because she was just another lady other than my mother. It made the whole weekend awkward because Abigail would kiss me, hug me, feed me, and treat me like my mother would treat me. She turned out to be a really nice lady.

After that weekend when my father brought me home to my mother late in the evening on Sunday, I was so happy to see her and quizzed her on what she cooked, as if I hadn't eaten with my father and Abigail all weekend. I think I was just trying to display my loyalty to her after spending the weekend with my father and my stepmother for the very first time. She also quizzed me as well about what my weekend was like with my father.

The weekend went by so quickly. When I got home, my chores had mounted up, and I still had to do my homework for school. My mother was having one of her living-room gatherings with about ten people when I walked into the house. Al Green's "Love and Happiness" was blaring out of the hi-fi stereo speakers to the smoke-filled room. Guests were sitting and dancing around the room, laughing and leaning over, whispering and holding conversations with one another—we had a rather lively household. My mother bought many records. She had Joe Tex, Aretha Franklin, James Brown, Etta James, etc.

That's when I couldn't help but notice that the people gathering at our house would always dress in a certain type of attire. There were these little green, black, and red flags sewn on their garments. They would dress in solidarity, adorned in symbolic clothing, accessorized with black beret hats, black leather coats, black pants, shirts, and military boots. It was also sort of a fashion statement. Although my mother wasn't a member, I later learned that these people were the same people that were called the Black Panther Party for Self-Defense. The Black Panthers believed that black people would truly not be free until they were able to determine their own destiny and objectives. Their ideology expanded and evolved rapidly throughout Watts.

CHAPTER 3

The atmosphere in Watts was a little uneasy due to the riots that were still simmering from 1965. The police would stop, search, and harass young black men for no apparent reason. Cops would selectively enforce the law when it came down to blacks in Watts. These practices led to tense relations between the police and the fed-up citizens. The unfair practices ignited a riot that exploded on the corner of 116th Street and Avalon. After what the police called a "routine stop," a citizen was badly beaten by several cops.

Less than a year after that civil unrest, two young black dudes by the name of Bobby Seale and Huey P. Newton formed the Black Panther Party in 1966 in Oakland, California. The Panthers actually stretched throughout the so-called ghettoes all over the United States of America. Police brutality remained a major issue in the black communities. The Panthers wanted to protect the black community from the unjust aggression of the police force.

Not only did they want to protect the community, they also wanted to serve the community. They would teach black pride and serve breakfast to the neighborhood kids at a house on 112th Street and Wilmington Avenue, across the street from my school, Grape Street Elementary. I would see them on the television news station protesting with guns in tow.

My mother believed in much of what the Black Panthers were teaching, such as black consciousness. She also saw the Black Panther Party as a village, and she often recited the old African proverb, "It takes a village to raise a child." So, naturally, she didn't mind me mingling with the Panthers' organization. However, the media did a good job of portraying the Panthers as haters of white people, when, in fact, the Panthers never accused any race as the oppressors. They always preached power to the people as their foundation because they felt that's what our country's democracy was all about, no matter what color you were in the establishment. But they were still portrayed as racist in the media in order to put fear in many white folks' minds, so whatever tactics used to destroy the Panthers' organization would be fair game in the eyes of many whites. Therefore, it was constant conflict between the police and the Black Panthers trying to maintain peace in the community.

The police in the community were the military arm of the establishment, so you have to expect them to try to protect the interests of the establishment. And in the process of protecting the establishment, some of the police felt, by the mere fact that young black men exist, they were a threat to the establishment. Some felt they had a right to destroy anything that threatened the establishment, as many of them were not there to protect us.

My mother would always preach to me about the "establishment." She felt that the establishment was set up to fail the black man if he wasn't twice as good as the next man.

When I would sometimes mess up in school and get a little "mannish," my mother called it, "smelling my ass." She would sometimes chastise me while holding a cigarette stuck in between her fingers with a long stem of ash barely hanging on it, while threatening to send me to my father's house. Then I would eventually straighten up, because I really didn't know what the outcome would be to that threat. Whenever my schoolwork wasn't up to her standards, she would tell me to use my head for more than a hat rack, insinuating that I wasn't using my head to think, but rather, just use it to wear hats. She encouraged me to study hard, and she rewarded me with delicious homemade desserts and stylish clothing.

My mother would derive good things from bad situations all the time by using her good mother's wit, and somehow, even without much help from my father, we didn't feel poor. We were far from rich, but I got a lot of love, and there were great sacrifices made on my mother's behalf, as I would see her struggling daily around the house.

Every weekend, I would wake up to the speeches of Malcolm X and Martin Luther King's eight-track tapes playing on the hi-fi stereo while she cleaned the house, the same hi-fi stereo she would use to entertain her friends with. Black pride was really pushed in our house. I didn't know if it was really in her heart or if it was just a way of getting back at my father for running off and marrying interracially. In any case, I got the idea of what she was saying or what she was pushing about the "establishment" in order to guide me on the right path.

CHAPTER 4

I thought I was headed up the right path . . . until I was moments from death. One morning I was experiencing something I couldn't understand. My mother entered my bedroom to get me going for school. I remember rocking back and forth on my bed, wheezing and coughing loudly. I couldn't breathe and pain was shooting all through my chest. I was crying and very scared, perhaps more so because I saw my mother in a panic; she seemed not to know what to do. She called some of the Panther members to take me to the Watts Clinic, and it was confirmed by Dr. Millicent Hill that I had asthma. I was diagnosed as a major asthmatic with a chronic lung condition. I was rushed into emergency surgery with a collapsed lung, and found out that the other one was on its way out, too. I was later moved to Martin Luther King Hospital, which was a larger facility than the Watts Clinic.

I was in the hospital for two weeks, lying in a small bed in what seemed like a very big room, all to myself. I was hooked up to oxygen tubes and a computer making beeping sounds all day as my lungs mended. I had a nurse, Matilda Goodrich, who was short and stocky, and she would jab this large needle in my arm really hard. I would yell out loud when she gave me the injection. One day my mother had a few words with her, and from then on, another nurse name Irene Jones, who was more helpful and assertive, would give me the shots. Every day, I would wake up with my mother sitting in a chair next to my bed. She devoted her time to nurturing me back to good health. She would help feed me my food, and then later help me out of bed to walk up and down the hallways of the hospital to regain my strength. She managed to help me pull through the pain of having my lung collapsed. She showed me what nurturing was all about.

Once I was able to leave the hospital and go home, my mother made me a German chocolate cake, and my friends and family members were there celebrating my coming home. She made me wear a baby Jesus pin every day to school as a child to keep me protected. My mother even made a big announcement as she quieted the room down and told everyone that due to my illness, she was quitting her smoking habit, which the doctor told her was the reason I had the chronic lung condition that caused the breathing problem. I also had to use an inhaler when I was playing outside due to dust and many other irritants that would trigger my breathing problems.

Some parts of the neighborhood had a vermin infestation of rodents and stray dogs, but Watts was so much fun that staying inside, even to protect my health, was not an option. There were many interesting things to do. Some of the guys raised pigeons in all different colors, and they would fly high and flip and tumble in the sky above the homes. It was like putting on an air show for the people. Some of the guys would play flag football against some of the neighboring guys from the Jordan Downs, Nickerson Gardens, and Imperial Courts projects—they played in big competitions. I used to go watch the games with my friend, Charlie Bradford. Charlie was a real light-skinned chubby dude with hazel eyes and curly sandy-brown hair. Some people would describe him as "the fat, high-yellow boy." We would get together and make go-cart coasters out of plastic milk crates with an old shoe skate nailed to the bottom. We would take the milk crates that the milkman would carry our milk bottles and dairy products in, and I don't know if it was against the law to use them, but we never got into any trouble. We played with them until the toy manufacturing company Mattel came out with the Big Wheel.

We also loved flipping on the old bed mattresses the neighbors would throw out for trash. But my mother wouldn't let me have the Big Wheel until I agreed to stay off the old mattresses. The Big Wheel was like a plastic tricycle with an oversized front wheel; it rides very low to the ground. The Big Wheel was a toy all the little boys on my street *had* to have for Christmas because the music group War had a song that had just come out, "Low Rider." The boys on my block thought the song was related to the Big Wheel. We all loved that song.

We rode our Big Wheels up and down the sidewalks of my street all day, into the late-evening hours, until the streetlights came on. That's when we knew we had to be in the house. We really couldn't let the streetlights come on and be caught outside the house. When that happened, our mothers would all yell for us to "get in the house."

We would sometimes play hide-and-go-seek. But when the girls on my street would play, Charlie would call it "hide-and-go-get-it." He liked hiding with the girls or going to go find them, and when he would find them or hide with them, he would start kissing them "if they let him." Charlie was really girl crazy.

I liked girls, too, but I was too shy and bashful to be crazy over them like he was. There was one girl, however, that made me light up whenever I would see her. She had these big brown eyes, two long ponytails, and pretty, long, skinny legs with caramel-colored skin. I think I had a love jones for her. I was sure we would make a good match, because I was a very slim, scrawny guy with dark chocolate skin and brown eyes sporting a huge Afro. Her name was Minda Myers, and I remember when Charlie and I had our first and last fight—it was over Minda.

One day while sitting on the porch of Charlie's house, I told Charlie my secret: that I liked Minda. And the very next day, Charlie went to school and went right up to Minda while she was playing tetherball with some of the other girls, and started to tease her about me liking her. Then he started pulling on one of her ponytails. Not only did he tell her my secret, but he also made her cry!

That's when I came to her rescue and got her out of imminent danger. I ran up to Charlie and popped him right in his mouth. I hit him in the mouth because that's where the words came from—when he knew good and well that I told him to keep the secret to himself. The fight started and ended in a wrestling match with the two of us rolling on the ground until my teacher, Ms. Chisholm, broke us up. Ms. Chisholm had us both write a hundred times, saying, "I will not strike my friend." It took about a day for us to make up.

CHAPTER 5

Summertime was always the best time because the neighborhood kids would walk to Will Rogers Park to swim and take swimming lessons. I think I didn't learn how to swim until I was about twelve years old. And many times on our way back home from swimming we would pick peaches and loquats off the trees in the backyards of houses along the way home because after swimming, we would have an appetite that was out of this world.

August was the month the Watts section of Los Angeless would put on a festival to commemorate the Watts riots back in the day. The Watts Festival was held at Will Rogers Park as well. Some people dressed in African garb. Many people would relax and spread out all through the park while sheltering themselves in the shade under the large pine trees.

There would be fair rides, vendors selling food, books, and artwork. Several well-known music and dance groups performed. You would see artists such as Isaac Hayes, the Watts 103rd Street Rhythm Band, Smokey Robinson and the Miracles. The Watts Prophets delighted the people by reciting poetry.

Those summer nights would feel so good. My mother would call them Indian summers, and you could just smell the wonderful scent of fruit trees and the jasmine bushes from miles around.

Throughout my childhood and into my preteens, I watched a change in the activities around the city. I saw the police come and raid some of the homes and have shootouts with the people from the village. Those same people used to come and visit at my house. Some of them ended up dead or convicted as political prisoners due to some of the FBI covert operations working in tandem with the local police.

There were dope dealers around the neighborhood, like this one particular small-time dope dealer guy by the name of Smitty, who would supply the neighborhood dope fiends . . . with the help of the cops on his payroll. The Black Panthers labeled him one of the worst kinds of guys around the neighborhood, and he was protected by the local law enforcement.

I've witnessed many of the people get hooked on some of the strongest drugs Smitty possessed. It was what they called LSD, or "acid." Some folks felt that the drugs had the village fragmented. It was also ruining the black pride in the city. Subsequently, the

Black Panther Party, once known for trying to make a difference in Watts, eventually disassembled, and the city went through a radical transformation from what the Black Panther Party had envisioned.

As we were approaching the mid- to late-seventies, my mother slowed down the preaching about the "establishment" and decided to connect with Saint Rest Baptist Church. It was a midsized church in South Central Los Angeles on the other side of town, presided over by the Reverend Dr. William Hill, pastor. Pastor Hill was an obese, dark-skinned, short man who stood about 5 foot 6. He would shout out Southern style while he preached. Pastor wore a toupee and had a gold tooth on the left side of his smile. I just knew one day that toupee would fall off while he was preaching. My mother became an usher and started singing in the choir. I used to love seeing her handling the church doors and working around the church. I took great pleasure in watching the people catch the Holy Ghost, running and shouting up and down the aisles.

When I was about thirteen years old, church was pretty cool to me. I attended Sunday school and Bible study, and while the stories in the Bible had me fascinated, the preaching would sometimes rattle me as a young man. So my mother would retell the stories to me, and in her own way, make many of them relevant to daily life. The teaching she gave me would make me feel good in some strange way.

She also gave me a little red Bible to keep in my pocket. I think it was called *The Personal Bible*. People would give them away to each other to read in good faith. Momma would always say, "You should give God some of your time," and I remember when I was a much younger boy, she got down on her knees with me at the side of my bed to teach me the Lord's Prayer. She made sure that I learned how to pray and knew how to trust and believe in God.

She told me to read this Bible whenever I wanted to or when I would feel uncertain about life, like, for instance, the time my uncle Sonny Boy was killed crossing the street on 105th and Central Avenue. Sonny Boy was my mother's brother. Whenever I crossed streets, the way he was killed always stayed with me.

Sonny Boy was crossing the street in the crosswalk. The first cars stopped to let him cross, while some guy drove around the other cars, I guess due to impatience, and went right through the crosswalk, hitting him and knocking him twenty feet into the air. Folks said that Sonny Boy landed on his head and snapped his neck.

He lay on his back in the middle of the intersection in a pool of blood, his eyes wide open looking up at the sky. He had a gaping head wound with blood oozing out. His life expired right there on the scene. It was unbelievable, and it left me shaken up about the whole ordeal when I heard about it.

After Sonny Boy's death, we spent about two weeks washing cars. Momma cooked and sold dinner plates to raise money to bury Sonny Boy just in time to still recognize him as he lay nestled in his powder-blue casket with white satin lining inside, dressed in his navy-blue suit. The funeral puzzled me because it was the first time I had attended a funeral. I was so moved by my family and friends' behavior with all the laughing and crying about Sonny Boy and recounting the things that he used to do. As they reminisced, I was baffled by how all these differing emotions could be expressed at once.

It took weeks for me to get over the fear about the traumatic incident, but I had to push on as a young man. My mother told me if I could describe my fears, then I could overcome them. She would continue making me attend church with her. She thought it would keep me grounded as she saw that I was going through some life changes.

When I didn't want to go to church I would pretend to be sick, and so my mother would not let me go outside on Sundays to play. She said if I was too sick to go to church, then I was too sick to go outside to play.

As a teenager, I thought I knew it all, like so many teenagers often do. Sometimes it seemed as though I could outsmart my mother, but I was always proven wrong.

CHAPTER 6

When I was attending Markham Junior High School, I breezed through my English and math courses, but I was barely getting by in my gym class due to my lack of participation, because I didn't like dressing in my gym shorts, showing my skinny legs—although I did enjoy exercising. I always hoped that all the exercises my PE teacher was putting me through would lead to a more muscular body. My asthma seemed to have stopped bothering me, and I found myself frequently leaving my inhaler at home until it was no longer a necessity for me. I was feeling healthier and stronger as my body was changing. Girls were always on my mind as I could recall begging my mother to let me attend my first school dance. She told me the only way she would let me go to the dance is if I went along with my friend Charlie and some of the guys that lived in my neighborhood.

My mother believed in safety in numbers; she thought that traveling within a group was better than traveling alone. She was always highly concerned about kidnappings, child molesters, and murders because the main topics on the television news stations were about the Patty Hearst abduction (she was a wealthy newspaper owner's daughter) and the Atlanta, Georgia, molestations and murders of young black boys. But being around a group of guys was something I never cared too much about.

So I told her that I was going to the dance with Charlie, and I would meet up with him at the corner of my street. But when I left the house, my real plan was to see if I could catch up with Maxine Baker. That was the girl in my homeroom class I liked because she seemed to be so smart and had nice long legs and a well-proportioned body, like a brick house or Coca-Cola bottle. I would just stare at her, especially when she wore her tight blue sweater with a plaid, pleated skirt, bobby socks, and those black-and-white shoes. She would have me feeling mesmerized, just like Minda Myers did when I was in elementary school until her family moved away out of state to Harlem, New York.

One afternoon when I was in class, I overheard Maxine talking to her cousin Linda about going to the dance, and I thought if I ran into Maxine on the way to the dance it would be good for me—also because I felt I would have the chance to be her first pick for the dance. You see, according to the school, it was the "Sadie Hawkins Day Dance." The Sadie Hawkins Day Dance is an unusual formal dance put on by the school, in which the female students invite the male students to the dance as their date. This is contrary to the custom of the male student inviting the female student to the school dance as their date. I never really knew or understood the history of Sadie Hawkins Day. Once at the dance, they would have a kissing booth available for the couples so they could go inside and kiss for about ten minutes.

So I left the house that evening wearing an orange and black dashiki shirt with brown corduroy bell-bottom pants coordinating with my black platform shoes. It was one of the same outfits I'd wear when I went to church with my mother. I also splashed on some of my mother's perfume just to have myself smelling like a rose. I ran about two blocks in the direction Maxine traveled to school, in hopes of running into her.

But my rushing was to no avail, so I ended up going to the dance alone. The dance was held in the school gymnasium, and the deejay was jamming. When I got to the dance, I saw Maxine, but by that time, she had already picked Clifford Whitfield as her date. I couldn't believe it. But I knew the only reason Clifford beat me to the punch was because he looked similar to and danced liked Little Michael Jackson. Man, was I jealous! I had thought she had eyes for me like I did for her. So I had no choice but to stick around and at least dance with Maxine's cousin, Linda; but I didn't want to be chosen by Linda. So I danced with her once to the song "Flash Light" by The Parliament, then I went over to see if I could find Charlie. Charlie had a date, so I decided to go back over to Linda. Linda and I danced all night, but she never actually chose me as her date. After the dance, Charlie walked home with his date, I walked with Linda, and Maxine walked with Clifford. For my mother's sake, I was traveling in a group.

When I approached age fifteen, I was really getting used to thinking on my own and learning the city; meanwhile, gangs were forming rapidly around Watts and in the Los Angeles area. In those days, safety was the first thought when leaving the house, as most of us had firsthand experience with crime.

I didn't realize how secure I was with being by myself at that time . . . until it created a problem for me. I was walking throughout one of the many vacant lots in the neighborhood, going to the corner store to get some Now & Laters and a Blow Pop sucker when about five dudes approached me telling me that they were the "new gang" in the neighborhood by the name of "The Runaway Slaves" (RAS). They said their gripe was with the white boys across the tracks in Lynwood, but they would still go out and commit robberies against some of the black folks in the neighborhood or get into squabbles with other black dudes in the city.

I was told when the gangs go out around the city to make themselves known they called it gangbanging. The Runaway Slaves actually gave me a choice to either join their gang or get my ass kicked and have my pocket change taken as well. So they put one of the young gangbangers up to fight me to pass through their gang initiation. I just stood there with an expression of disbelief on my face, while analyzing the gang members before I could make my decision, as I was compelled to make a choice. The young gangbanger went into a fighting stance, so I started clenching my fists. That's when another member of the gang interrupted the fight before it even had gotten started.

It was Big Rufus, my friend Charlie's big brother. Big Rufus was a huge fella, all muscles; at age eighteen, he stood about 6 foot 2 and weighed maybe 200 pounds. He had a red complexion with dark brown freckles all over his face, and he wore his hair in big thick cornrows from front to back. He recognized me as Charlie's friend and suggested that the gang stall me out and let me go on my way. I walked away and sighed with relief, knowing my mother was right; I could hear her telling me that I shouldn't have had my ass out there traveling alone. But we were still at odds on how to travel throughout the city as a young man. I felt if I was traveling with a group of guys, there's a possibility we would have been mistaken as a gang, and the ordeal might have gotten a little violent without having Big Rufus there. He didn't take shit from anybody. I once witnessed him knock a guy out with one punch before the fight even started. He would fight two and three dudes at a time. He admitted to Charlie and me that he would get excited to fight the loudmouthed, boisterous, obnoxious dudes because he had a disdain for those kinds of guys.

The gangs had replaced the Black Panther Party in my neighborhood as the Panthers' ideas had eroded over time in the minds of the gangs. And I couldn't understand some of the reasons for which they were fighting. But it looked like Big Rufus was running the gang in my neighborhood. The Black Panther Party taught the kids in Watts values and had a purpose back in the day; the RAS gang didn't have a rhyme or reason for many of the things they were doing, so they had me confused, and I couldn't stand being confused or mixed up because I had such an analytical mind.

My mother warned me to stay away from the RAS gang, and I was more afraid of my mother than the influences outside my house. I basically became a pacifist. My mother felt that the RAS gang was a bunch of socially engineering criminals. She would refer back to her black consciousness to say the gangs turn the victims into willing accomplices to help in the extermination of their own people. She said that the gangs were cursed with petty indifferences, and they fought about fabricated concepts in believing that they actually owned the turf that they were fighting over. She would therefore express her concerns about the community and tell me you can easily damage the community by destroying its children; you get to the boy and you get to the girl, and the future will be over. She also said the people are only as good as their seed, explaining her strict protection of me. Therefore, I would try to steer myself away from the gangs. As the RAS gang had a strong hold in Watts, with Big Rufus leading the pack, they eventually took over Smitty's dope operation and chased him out of town over into Hollywood, where he had a large clientele of Hollywood actors and "upper-class people."

By this time, the city slowed down with putting on the Watts festivals as the surrounding cities became excessively violent with young men annihilating one another, leaving the mothers pleading to the indifferent local politicians for help—only to see them change their attitude around election time.

Under my mother's guidance to help push and pull me through that environment, she would always monitor my friends. She didn't mind Charlie because we had come up together as small kids, and Charlie was focused more on the girls than on getting into trouble.

But I would often see guys behaving differently and doing things in a gang or a group that they wouldn't normally do by themselves, masquerading, pretending to be someone they were not. The gangs had a big influence on many of the young guys who didn't have their fathers around, just like the Black Panthers had on the young guys back in the day. I noticed over half of the guys on Hickory Street didn't have their fathers at home due to their parents breaking up, their fathers being in jail, or their fathers being dead. Some of us would mention or discuss our fathers while hanging out on the street, signifying and playing the dozens.

I guess being the only child was how I obtained my self-confidence without the help of a group or a gang. I can recall Kenneth Potts, this tall, slinky guy in my sixth-period class in ninth grade. He was picking on me and teasing me about my weight because I was a real skinny dude. He had the whole class cracking up about how small my arms were. So when the bell rang, I followed him into the restroom. I caught him with his pecker out using the stall. I walked right up to him and threatened to kick his ass for cracking jokes about my arms. I really wanted to fight him right then and there, but he just stared at me like I was crazy, then began to apologize. He may have thought that it was an awkward moment, but I was quite upset. I never had a problem with Kenneth about my arms again after that restroom visit.

CHAPTER 7

I recall when one summer was slowly approaching and the local radio station commercials were announcing the last Watts Festival's lineup and headliners. The community was very excited about seeing celebrities, while the temperature was reaching one of the highest recorded in the city.

On this one particular day, Charlie, a dude name Reggie, and I were hanging out when a car pulled up to the curb. The driver leaned over to ask us if we were interested in work, and we all jumped at that opportunity. We were anxious to have the chance to make some money. He was a white guy with strawberry blond hair and little beady blue eyes and gold-framed glasses who introduced himself as Peter. He resembled the actor Robert Redford, but with very pale skin. He said that he was riding around the neighborhood looking for guys who wanted to work. Reggie asked Peter what his last name was. He told us Peter Stevenson was his name, but emphatically, without question, told us to call him Peter. Peter drove a 1979 tan Ford station wagon, and he had stacks of encyclopedias in the back. He told us that we would be selling the encyclopedias door to door for forty dollars a set, and we would get twenty dollars from each sale. We all gladly agreed.

Peter said that he would pick us up the next day after school. We waited for Peter the next day. He came and took us across town through some of the upscale neighborhoods toward Hollywood. We were just happy about going over into that part of the town. But then I got nervous because I didn't tell my mother about the job, let alone tell her about Peter. I told Peter midway across town that I had to stop at the nearest phone booth to call my mother. He told me that I would be able to use the phone at his house because he had to stop to get more encyclopedias. Charlie said that he would need to call his mother as well, but Reggie said his mother got home late at night and that his father didn't care, as long as Reggie wasn't at home getting on his nerves.

Peter drove us to his house in West Hollywood. That was the first time any of us had ever gone to Hollywood, even though it's only twenty minutes away from Watts. The only fascinating place I had been at the time was to the Watts Towers, which is located in the heart of Watts. The towers are made out of concrete, tile, and glass that make them unique and beautiful pieces of artwork.

Peter lived alone in this big brown house on Harper Avenue, a quiet, tree-lined street near Santa Monica Boulevard. When we got into the house and before I could use the phone, the first thing

Peter did was offer us a beer. Reggie was a little older than Charlie and I, and we never had a beer before, but Reggie had, so Reggie helped himself and took a bottle of beer out of the refrigerator. Charlie noticed that Peter had a stack of *Playboy* and *Playgirl* magazines. And Charlie, being girl crazy, had his eyes stuck in those magazines. I had never seen magazines like those before. Hell, at that time, I had never seen a naked girl before, so although I was a little bashful, I began sweating and looking at the naked ladies in the pictures right alongside Charlie.

Time went by and I realized that Reggie was drinking his third beer, and Charlie and I were still immersed in the enjoyment of those magazines for about an hour. We were very excited to be in Hollywood, looking at naked women, and drinking beer. We forgot about Peter until he returned wearing only a robe. Peter walked over to Charlie and I while we were sitting on the couch with our faces glued to the pages in the magazines.

He sat right between the two of us and asked us if we liked what we saw. I was thinking he was talking about the women in the magazines. Then he put his hands on each of our thighs and began to spread his legs, exposing his pecker to us both.

Charlie and I looked up at each other at the same time and before we could say a word, Reggie came out of nowhere and stumped Peter right in his nuts while he was sitting there, then he whacked him across the head with his beer bottle.

The bottle broke and split open a deep cut on Peter's forehead. Blood was gushing out everywhere. Reggie hit Peter repeatedly with both fists until Reggie had blood all over his hands and shirt.

He still had the broken bottleneck griped tightly in his hand. Peter was beaten and cut so badly that Charlie and I were screaming at Reggie to stop as we pulled him off Peter.

I just knew Reggie had killed him. Reggie ordered us to find Peter's keys as he ran over to the kitchen sink to wash the blood off his hands, but he couldn't get rid of the blood on his shirt. I found the keys and gave them to Reggie, and he headed for the door. Charlie and I were on his tail, and we never looked back. Reggie got behind the wheel, and I jumped in the passenger seat with Charlie in the backseat.

Reggie drove down Santa Monica Boulevard, speeding like a bat out of hell, and that's when the Hollywood police pulled us over with their lights and sirens sounding. The cops escorted each of us out of the car and onto the sidewalk, then had us all sit on the curb with our hands in handcuffs behind our backs. The first cop asked Reggie for his driver's license, just when the second cop asked Reggie where he got all the blood on his shirt. As he ignored the second cop's question, he told the first cop that he left his license at home, when he really didn't have one at all. The second cop repeated his question with anger.

Then the first cop asked him where he lived as they took turns questioning Reggie. Before he could tell them, a call came through on their car radio to report a stolen tan Ford station wagon along with three young black males. Peter must have regained consciousness and called the police on us. So we were taken to jail and booked.

Although we were teenagers, the cops wanted to charge us as adults, due to the severe beating Reggie gave Peter. Peter also made a statement indicating that we all beat him in order to trump up the charges against us.

We all were charged with assault and grand theft auto. The cops gave us our one phone call to our mothers, but we still had to stay in jail for seventy-two hours. Those hours seemed like an eternity.

The police separated us during the time we were in jail, so I was alone in this cage, and all I could hear was constant keys jiggling and barred doors opening and slamming. My only visit was the guards coming to bring me my meals. I would finally force myself to sleep, and if I had a pleasant dream about Maxine or something like that, I'd eventually wake up looking at those gray-colored, cold, steel bars that held me confined until Reggie told the cops that he was responsible for both of the charges. I couldn't believe Reggie took the whole rap, but I was glad at the same time.

My mother had to catch a cab to the jail alone because Charlie's mother told him that if he ever landed in jail, she would never get his ass out. So my mother took us both home, and when I told her the whole story she still grounded me because I never took the time to call her that day until I was locked up.

Reggie was sentenced to one year in Juvenile Hall Detention Center, California Youth Authority, by the judge, but he was also called a hero because Peter turned out to be a pedophile. Peter was considered an intelligent man, but was labeled a loner with a checkered past as some of the guys in the neighborhood testified against him as a child molester. Nevertheless, Reggie was still charged with an "overzealous" assault. I guess they had to come up with an offense on the young black boy, but then the charge became what's known as a "DA reject" and subsequently was dropped.

CHAPTER 8

h

As my first growth of fuzz started to develop under my nose and on my upper lip, I had a growth spurt, which landed me at 5 foot 6 and 120 pounds with a little meat on my arms. At the same time, the city I called my hometown was going through a drastic change in characteristics with many of the vacant lots made into shopping centers, leaving the Watts Towers still the most fascinating structure in the city. The Los Angeles Rams found another hometown—and boy!—my mother was extremely upset about that whole ordeal until a few years later the Los Angeles Raiders came in from Oakland, California, blazing, winning our love for them, as Southern California became the new Raiders country. The Raiders team had gangbangers to grandmothers wearing their Raiders gear. The Los Angeles Coliseum was the hottest place to be at game time.

Meanwhile, I was in my last year of junior high school. I realized my mother needed some help around the house, and I'm not talking about cooking and cleaning, but money to help with the bills. My father would come by once in a blue moon to slide my mother a few bucks, but it wasn't much. Therefore, as we were having one of our movie-night dinner fests where we ate pizza, followed by ice cream, which was my favorite meal, I asked my mother to allow me to get a small job at the local ABC market as a bag boy. I knew some of the boys in my neighborhood were making money by bagging groceries; she gladly obliged me.

George Clinton's Parliament-Funkadelic, along with Bootsy Collins, were tearing down the Inglewood Forum in sold-out concerts. O. J. Simpson was the hottest celebrity in television commercials for Hertz Rental Car, running through the airport jumping over luggage. He was America's football hero. Muhammad Ali was still the heavyweight champion of the world before relinquishing the title to Leon Spinks.

I felt really good about making money and trying to help out. It gave me a sense of pride, just like what the Black Panthers Party was preaching about. But I won't forget the first time I got paid. I was walking home from work on the back streets of Santa Ana along the train tracks near the Watts Towers. I was feeling quite proud of myself when, lo and behold, there came these two dudes that didn't look too familiar. These dudes caught up with me, and all I could think about was what my mother had told me about traveling alone. At that point, I knew all I had to count on was that little red Bible my mother gave me, and my faith in God to get me home and through this situation safely. These dudes were rough, and one of them asked me if I had any money. Before I could say anything, the other dude was going through my pockets, and when I pulled back to get his left hand out of my pocket, he hit me with the right in my left jaw, and I hit the ground. They robbed me of my first paycheck, and when I finally made it home to tell my mother, she took me to the Watts Health Foundation Clinic on 103rd Street. I was examined and treated, then released by Dr. Millicent Hill. We later learned that she was the head doctor of the clinic, with a kind and caring personality. I guess it was in her blood because she was also the sister of Reverend William Hill. I was happy to survive the whole ordeal with all my teeth intact.

My mother suggested that I start catching the bus to work; so I needed to borrow some money from her to buy a bus pass to get to work a little faster and safer; and to travel with a crowd. I caught the Rapid Transit District bus to work. RTD was the acronym for the company. Once I started catching the bus to work, I was making it to work ahead of my schedule, which gave me the opportunity to train for other job duties, such as cashier, and it allowed me to get a promotion with a pay increase. I was feeling like a real man, although I was still just a teenager. I was fifteen years old and starting to attend Jordan High School, focusing on my studies. My most interesting subject was geography; the study of lands, their features, and the inhabitants has always fascinated me—besides studying the female student body that was seated next to me in class.

While working at ABC, I made some small changes to my appearance. I got rid of my Afro and traded it in for a Jheri curl hairstyle. Life around me was going through many changes: Afros went into Jheri curls, and R&B went from disco into hip-hop/rap music. Bell-bottoms pants went to Levi's jeans; corduroy pants to baggy jeans and slacks. We put the dashiki shirts away and put on the Polo shirts or the dress shirts with the skinny ties.

Now that I kept hip-hop and rap music playing on my mother's hi-fi, I fell in love with the hip-hop/rap group Sugarhill Gang's song "Rapper's Delight." I started trying to write my own rhymes. I'd sing that rap song going to school and coming back home from school. During those days, I eventually made a couple of truces with a couple of my old rivals, Clifford Whitfield and Kenneth Potts, only because Kenneth heard me spitting my rap, and he knew Clifford could rap, too, and Kenneth was an okay rapper himself, and we all loved hip-hop music. So Kenneth thought that it would be a good idea for the three of us to get together and form a hip-hop/rap group and enter the school's upcoming talent show. We would call ourselves the Sugarhill Gang and do the rap song "Rapper's Delight." We all agreed that Clifford would rap the part of "Wonder Mike," Kenneth would rap the part of "Big Bank Hank," and I would rap the part of "Master Gee."

And, man! We blew the roof off the place after that talent show. We got so much recognition from the whole school—even the teachers! Everyone was telling us that we should really form a rap group. We played around with the idea for a while, but once all the recognition died down and as the school year moved on, the desire went away. I continued to write my rhymes and everybody would call me a rapper, but I didn't have a group.

I just knew I was *the man*—until I came home one day and opened the door, and to my surprise, I saw Charles Thomas, the neighborhood fabric man, sitting on my mother's couch. He sold sewing fabric door to door in Watts. But this time, he was not selling fabric. Charles was a tall, handsome guy with a bronze-brown ebony skin tone with a processed hairstyle. Because he dressed in his tailor-made suits, I took him for a bourgeois type of fellow. He was sitting real close to my mother—almost too close. I didn't pay too much attention to my mother during the times Charles would come by selling sewing fabric. But my mother would buy fabric all the time, and Charles would come by almost every other weekend. My mother had a trunk full of fabric, but she hadn't sewn a thing. Heck, she didn't even have a sewing machine!

I should have known, but instead, I was more preoccupied with trying to keep up with the Jordan High School cheerleaders and trying to be the coolest dude in school.

I would see Charles at my house every weekend after that. My mother would prepare special dinners for him when he would come by to visit. I guess you would say that he was my mother's boyfriend at the time. He and I never had too much interaction or talks; he never tried to tell me about the birds and the bees or any of that stuff. Charles would make Momma laugh, and she would seem so happy when he came by. Momma was very careful how she behaved in front of me, but I was glad to see Momma happy in that way. Then there were times when Momma would appear so upset; suddenly Charles wasn't around anymore. My mother kept a picture of my father beside her bed. I suppose she had never quite gotten over him.

There were other courtships for a few years, but nothing serious, I suppose. Some of the wooing left my mother with major mood swings, and the relationships would just end.

Momma would lecture me about how to treat the girls that I thought I liked, like Maxine. She would always tell me to lay my cards on the table, remain respectful, and be sincere to them—even if it cost me the relationship.

I would listen to the things she had to say, but by that time, I thought I knew all about the subject of girls, because I had studied them all through middle school. And during my midteens, I had a storm building inside of me—I had to finally surrender to my hormones. I discovered a desire to please myself, and masturbation was like the best thing invented to feed my imagination.

Once I was in my second year of high school with a job, the only thing that I was missing was a car to be voted "most wanted boyfriend in school." But a car was out of the picture at that time because I needed to be seventeen and a half to get my driver's license, and I was only sixteen going on seventeen. I was breezing through my studies as gym was becoming the coolest class because my weight started to increase and my push-up exercises gave my arms muscle mass. I also enjoyed watching the girls exiting the locker room and entering the gym field.

Prince and Michael Jackson were burning up the pop music charts, along with video music channels on televisions around the world. "Little Red Corvette" and "Billie Jean" were playing everywhere you turned. My mother and I would sit up late at night eating ice cream and watching ON television or Select television when the new cable television was introduced.

CHAPTER 9

W̶hen I reached my senior year of high school with a B-plus overall grade, my mother had an idea to enroll me into the busing school program, which allowed me, along with other inner-city black students, to attend a basically all-white high school in the suburbs of the large cities, and vice versa. Well, that was the way it was designed to work, but most of the white students didn't enroll in the so-called black schools. When we were enrolling into their schools, many of the white families moved their children into private schools in so-called white flight, which reduced the effectiveness of the program. By the time I was signed up for the program, it was on its last leg.

The busing program was an experiment in desegregating the somewhat still segregated school system of the early days of the United States school system until the ruling in 1954 when the U.S

Supreme Court, in the *Brown v. Board of Education* case, declared racial segregation in public school unconstitutional. The school district provided zero-fare bus transportation to and from my assigned school. I was assigned to Van Nuys High School.

My mother's idea for me to attend a school in Van Nuys didn't sit well with me at the beginning; however, she convinced me to try it, thinking it may give me a little more life exposure. She was right. It was a stark contrast to Jordan High, and I was a black boy from the inner city enrolled in an elective class with the title of Future Farmers of America, which had us studying the farm lifestyle with livestock working the land. The school had a swimming pool, and thank God for the Will Rogers Park swimming pool back in my city. I made the swim team, but my favorite course was political science, a social science discipline concerned with the study of the state, nation, government, and politics. Regarding governmental policies, it was so surprising to learn how much of a role the black people could play in the science that makes our country run.

As I took the good, I had to take the bad along the way. Although it seemed as if I'd escaped the inner city gangs as a distraction, instead, I fell right into the hands of the white racist antics and jokes from some of the students. It was a real eye-opener for me at the time because that was my first time to encounter white boys pulling racist pranks with malice. I was ill prepared for the racial prejudice I encountered; therefore, just as I had done with Kenneth Potts back in the day, I had to ambush this one particular blond-haired, green-eyed big bully named Chad Austin on the wrestling team. They called him C. A. in school. As he was leaving the gymnasium from his wrestling class, I had to put a stop to the "blackface," "watermelon," and "go back to Africa" jokes. I didn't catch him alone, so I had to borrow a baseball bat from the sports equipment closet in the gym.

I caught C. A. and two of his friends in the locker room shower as they were finishing up one of their wrestling matches. I made sure they were alone as I took their towels and clothes while they were showering. I had them cornered with only soap, water, and the good sense to help get them out of the difficult situation they suddenly found themselves in. I allowed his two friends to leave as I felt a need to talk to C. A. alone; so I handed the two guys their clothes. Chad started to try to bargain with me in front of his friends to smooth out the predicament, and the mere fact that he broke down apologizing in front of his peers satisfied me enough, so I made them leave in a hurry. Once they were on their way out, I thought I'd just make C. A. flinch a little, so I raised the bat up over my shoulder, menacing him like a batter at the plate—until I flashed a grin like he did when he was making those racist remarks to me. I had him put on his clothes and told him to keep away from me.

Nonetheless, throughout the school year, I would still encounter racial tension. And the school was still segregated unless they were having a sporting event like a football game, basketball game, or a school dance. It was just like a microcosm of the country; sporting events and music were sure to erase the racial lines.

Just when I got a personal perspective on how some of the other people in the world behaved, high school was coming to an end with prom time just a week away, and then I would be off looking forward to graduation. I mustered up the nerve to ask Jocelyn Danford in my math class to be my date for the prom. She accepted my offer. I guess I was infatuated with her, and I really was excited to have Jocelyn as my date. Jocelyn had pretty caramel-brown skin, stood about 5 foot 2, was 120 pounds, and had a nice booty with cute corkscrew curls at shoulder length. She was a thick-legged girl with lovely brown eyes and big hips that made her backbone slip as her body swayed in a really nice way when she walked. She was also one of the few girls who had her own car in high school. She drove a 1978 gold Chevy Camaro. I was happy as I could be.

The next time I got paid from work, I asked Charlie to ride downtown with me to rent a tuxedo for the prom, but he declined because he wanted to go over to his girlfriend's house because her parents weren't home, and he thought it was his chance to get "lucky" with her.

I ended up catching the RTD bus downtown by myself, and I could just hear my mother yelling at me about traveling alone. So I ignored the voice in my head in order to get downtown, because I felt I had to get my tuxedo.

I went ahead and waited for the bus, and when the bus arrived, I got on and showed my bus pass, then I headed to the back since the ride would take about forty-five minutes to get downtown. I thought that I'd make myself comfortable, so I happened to sit on the bench seat facing the window just before the very last seat in the back, because that seat was occupied with these two dudes. I couldn't help but notice that they had begun to play a card game with just three cards as soon as I sat down in my seat.

I started to watch the game they were playing, and the game seemed simple enough. The dealer guy would shuffle the cards, and the other guy would place a bet with his money to see if he could find the red ace, and if not, he would lose the money that he bet. The guy that was placing his bet down continued to win. The guys saw that I was watching intensely, so they invited me to play the game and place a bet to find the red ace. I knew I had just gotten paid, and the money I had was for my tuxedo to go to the prom. So I was a little reluctant to place my money down and make a bet. Then the guys together convinced me to play by making a bet with just five dollars of my money. I thought this would be a good chance for me to make some extra money.

I took five dollars out of my pocket and made my bet while the guy showed me the faces of the cards. Then he shuffled the cards and lined them up face down on the seat of the bus. It was my turn to pick out the red ace out of the three cards. I picked the card, and to my luck, I picked the red ace. I played two more times straight and won each time. Then I was getting excited, and there were other bus passengers gathering around, so I was feeling lucky and thinking that there was no way I could lose at this game.

Therefore, I placed more of my money down, and I won again, so I thought that I would place just about all my money down. By this time, I was fully involved in the game. Then the tables turned . . . for the worse. I started to lose a large portion of my money—fast. I felt I needed to get back on the winning streak. But I was losing. I raised my head to look out the front window of the bus to see if the bus was approaching my stop, and sure enough, Seventh and Broadway was the stop that was next to come.

I was still losing my money, and the dealer had a lot of my tuxedo money in his pocket by now. I started to sweat profusely, so I thought that I'd take my last chance and place all the money down that I had left in my pockets on this last bet before the bus reached Seventh and Broadway. The dealer guy shuffled the cards this last time, and with my mind racing and face full with beads of sweat, I stared at the cards while he laid them out on the seat. He looked up at me and said, "Okay, take your pick."

My face was sweaty, and my hands were too. I started to bite down on my bottom lip, and then I reached out, grabbed the middle card, and flipped it over. To my dismay, I grabbed the queen of clubs. I looked up at the guy, and he said to me, "Better luck next time," and before I could speak a word, the bus driver yelled out, "Seventh and Broadway!" I stood up with hesitation followed by a blank stare and walked slowly as the back doors opened up to allow me to exit the bus. I left without a cent. I only had my bus pass in my pockets.

I felt like someone had taken me by my feet and turned me upside down to shake the money out of my pockets. I got off the bus, and I just stood there looking around as if I was lost. Then I decided to walk up and down the streets. I had an ax to grind with the world, but I was more pissed off with myself to allow those guys to lure me in with that simple game of cards.

I caught the bus back home, thinking of a story to tell my mother, Jocelyn, and Charlie. I had to make it good, because I didn't want to look like the fool that I was. I went home and told my mother that I lost the money somewhere on the bus, which wasn't actually a story. When I saw Charlie, I broke down and told him the whole story; he then told me that it was a scam card game his brother Big Rufus would play on people to get their money. It was called "Three Card Monte" and only played by con men.

My next problem was how to tell Jocelyn that I could not go to the prom, because I didn't have a tuxedo. I didn't want to ask my mother for the money to get the tuxedo, because she was already struggling to make ends meet. I felt like a loser and irresponsible, squandering and losing my money. I told Jocelyn that I was sick, and I could not go to the prom. I ditched her and my classes all week, faking my illness. Jocelyn ended up going to prom with Lamar Reynolds, leaving me both relieved and disappointed.

I learned a serious lesson about hustlers and traveling alone. I figured I needed to save my money and get a car as soon as I came of age. But if I did have a car at the time, I would have been the most vulnerable young man in high school because I was still a virgin, and I remained a virgin throughout high school. Although I had a couple of close calls on losing my virginity, I did not have luck like my buddy Charlie did.

CHAPTER 10

As I survived the Los Angeles Unified School system, it was time to put it to the test. This was my first summer in the free world. I didn't feel immediate pressure, as I was still working. Although there were some uncertainties moving around inside me from time to time, telling myself I'm an adult now, I was not sure what that really meant, because in an adult world, it can get a little spooky.

Therefore, my first summer out of school as an adult was very exciting. Charlie and I would hit all the local parties, and we would go to Hollywood and just hang out on Hollywood Boulevard, watching the girls and flirting all night. However, I could never get lucky with any of the girls that I would meet.

When I was nineteen years old, I can remember my first sexual experience as I approached manhood, and it was nothing like what

Big Rufus would tell Charlie and me. Maybe all the nervousness and uncertainty made my whole experience a little weird. The girl turned out to be Linda Baker; yes, Maxine Baker's cousin, the same girl I tried to go the Sadie Hawkins dance with back in the day. I happened to bump into Linda on Imperial and Figueroa at the Nix check cashing. It was the second of July, and when I first saw Linda, she didn't remember me. She was looking so fine, even though I liked her cousin Maxine back in the day. I felt that we were just kids, but now, I had seen what the woman Linda had become, with chocolate skin as if her body was tanned from heaven. I didn't think it mattered if I had a schoolboy crush on her cousin years ago. So I walked up to her, and I said, "Hey, girl, you're still looking fine as ever!" She looked at me and turned her nose up at me as if she never knew me and as if that was just some cheap pickup line.

I started over again and introduced myself as Nathaniel Smith from Markham Junior High School from back in the day. She couldn't recollect my name or my face, although it had been many years since we'd seen each other. It took some time to jog her memory.

In any case, I asked her about her cousin, Maxine, and she told me that Maxine wasn't doing too good these days and that she was lost and turned out working on Century Boulevard and Prairie Avenue as a prostitute due to her drug addiction. Maxine had married a dude named Randy from Compton with two kids, and once they were married and the relationship was on the rocks, they started experimenting with marijuana mixed with cocaine when times got rough for them both. Randy later kicked the habit and tried to become a drug dealer as his wife Maxine became hooked on his product. He was subsequently busted and sent to Soledad State Prison for ten years; meanwhile, their kids were living over in the city of Carson with Maxine's parents.

Linda said that Maxine had a pimp by the name of Solomon who worked his prostitutes in that location because of all the action that was going on due to Inglewood Forum with the Lakers basketball games and horse racing at the Hollywood Race Track.

She said Solomon would have three to four prostitutes at a time from his stable working Prairie Avenue, and he would often beat them up and down the streets if their money was short of what it should have been for that night. They would walk the streets as he drove his 1978 souped-up brown Cadillac Seville with all the trimmings on it, sporting white wall tires and Daytona rims. He would dress as an outdated pimp from the seventies with his big hat and red polyester jumpsuit under a long leopard fur coat. And he had a grandiose attitude to top it all off.

We talked for a few hours. Soon our conversation went in a more provocative direction, and during those few hours, the exchange developed into a deep crush for each other.

At that time, ABC Market had gone out of business, and I had just started to work for Zodys Department Store. I used to cashier and stock the shelves at the store on Crenshaw and Century in Inglewood. I also bought myself a black and gold Datsun B-210, and, man, I was ready for anything!

I took down her phone number and called her the next day, which I later learned wasn't what a guy should do for some reason, but I thought if I liked the girl, why not call her the first chance I got?

We talked on the phone all night until Linda and I thought it would be nice for us to get together the next day for the Fourth of July holiday. We met up over at her family's house in Carson; they lived on Avalon Boulevard and Del Amo Boulevard. We had a ball. Then Linda thought that it would be cool for us to go get a room at the Holiday Inn on Vermont and 190th Street in the next city over in Torrance. I really didn't want to go because there was a part of me that wasn't quite sure what we were going there for.

I was trying to get myself together before we got to the hotel. I didn't know how to rent the room, and I wasn't certain if I was the one that should go up to the desk and buy the room. So when I drove into the hotel parking lot and parked my car, we sat there in the car for a moment until I could feel Linda looking at me as I was wrapped up in deep thoughts.

She asked if I was going to get out and get the room, as if she was in a rush. I quickly turned my head in her direction and looked her in the eyes and said, "Oh yeah, I'm on my way in now." I got out of the car, walked into the hotel, and headed for the front desk.

There was a lady working alone behind the desk. She looked at me and said, "Hello, are you checking in?"

I said, "Uh, yeah, I would like to get a room."

"How many days would you like to occupy the room?"

"For maybe just an hour."

"You cannot rent a room for an hour because we are not a motel."

I thought to myself, what in the hell was the difference? A room for rent was just a room for rent.

"You will have to rent the room for the remainder of the night or a day."

I didn't think we needed a room for the whole day, so I got the room for the remainder of the night. Once I paid the money for the room and received the key, I returned to the car. Linda immediately grabbed the key out of my hand, jumped out of the car, and headed toward the room. I followed her to room 110. That's when all the exhilaration started, and my heart sped up into a full gallop.

Linda was a little more experienced in the intimate field, and intimacy was obviously on her mind. You could say she taught and showed me all the moves and ways to go. As we sat down on this large California king-sized bed, and the bed itself was quite intimidating, we started off chatting a little as she proceeded to undress, while I carefully watched her disrobe. And I'll tell you, Linda had a good-looking body, like the women in those magazines Charlie and I looked at years ago.

I went into speaking ambiguous gibberish to quiet my anxiety until I was the only one fully clothed. Then she leaned over to me and placed her whole mouth over my lips, thrusting her tongue almost down my throat in order to shut me up.

She took my hands and placed them both over her breasts as she instructed me to rub and squeeze her nipples. Then she reached for my belt buckle to unbuckle my pants. She unzipped my zipper, then began tugging my pants downward. I felt simultaneously helpless and aroused.

I jumped up quickly and pulled my pants all the way off along with my Fruit of the Loom tighty whities. Then I sat on the edge of the bed beside her. Once I was fully naked, she forced me backward and climbed on top of me. I thought to myself that this is what Adam and Eve must have looked like. Her nipples were rock hard and pointed, and for a moment, I wasn't sure if I had enough of what Linda wanted, knowing that this wasn't her first time around.

I guess I was up to standards by her actions when she took her hand and grabbed my pecker, enhancing my erection and instructing me on how to penetrate her vagina repeatedly with thrusting, as she applied a gentle, steady stroking motion with her hips and midsection. Her performance sent me into an out-of-body experience. We entered into a crescendo as we both began to moan out loud with heavy breathing, until there was a sudden silence near the beginning of a slow climax as emotions filled the room.

The intercourse continued periodically in various positions throughout the night with erotic thrusting until checkout time, leaving us both happily satisfied. Needless to say, I found joy in repetition. It was terrific and terrifying, all at the same time. As a guy, I felt I should have taken the lead in the whole situation, but that had not been the case.

Linda and I dated for a while. We loved going to the movies. Our favorite movie was *9½ Weeks* with Mickey Rourke and Kim Basinger. If we weren't together, we would be on the phone throughout the night, into the wee hours of the morning. Just like many couples, we had our ups and downs; we would argue about things we just could not shake about each other.

We both had our issues. The problem Linda had with me was that she felt I was what they called a "Momma's Boy" because I would often quote my mother, and frequently compare Linda to her whenever we'd be out on a date or when we had a problem in the relationship. She would tell me that she was going to send me back to my mother one day, although we weren't even living together.

The problem I had with Linda was that when we went out, she would often dress in revealing clothing because she loved the attention she would get from the other guys. That, along with her flirting, caused many problems for me, and I would end up in an altercation with several guys around town when I was with her.

I must admit I was a little insecure when it came down to our relationship, because I knew Linda was unconventional, according to my mother's explanation of how a good girl should be.

I thought that we really loved each other through our ups and downs. At least I thought I loved her, but then, maybe it was just a case of me being hooked on what I thought was love due to Linda taking my virginity—as I indicated, Linda was a little more advanced than I. You see, Linda was the kind of girl who liked to give her vagina away, as if it were a sandwich she didn't want. The whole relationship was like reading a good book. Although I loved all the excitement that was happening in every chapter, I just couldn't help but wonder how this good book would end.

The ending was revealed to me when I caught her cheating on me.

One evening, Charlie and I took a cruise around downtown Los Angeles near the movie theaters on Ninth and Broadway when I saw Linda on a date all hugged up with this big bodybuilder dude. Man, dude was twice my size; his arms were the size of my thighs. They were laughing and carrying on. Linda looked right directly in my eyes. It was written all over her face that this guy she was with had taken my place. She didn't have to say a word, and all I could do was stare as my heart filled with despair. I was unable to speak through my emotions. At this burning moment of anger and humiliation, I was so mortified and furious my stomach went into knots, and all of a sudden, I broke out into a heavy sweating episode. Then Charlie started speaking to me, and I couldn't comprehend anything he was saying. I thought to myself, I better get home because I was feeling sick and brokenhearted. Charlie drove me home because I could barely see my way through the tears in my eyes.

I knew Linda was promiscuous, but at the time, it was good for me because I was with her. But once the shoe was on the other foot, it didn't feel too good. I guess she toyed with my love. I became a victim of circumstance.

I knew Linda was seeing some other guy because she was never home. Charlie tried to tell me on many occasions when I could never catch Linda at home, but I didn't want to accept it. When I would try to contact her to arrange a date, her mother would always tell me that she was out with friends. I guess you could say she dumped me. I was looking forward to going home and sharing the disenchanted feelings I'd gained regarding Linda with my mother.

CHAPTER 11

Charlie and I returned home from cruising, and I put my key in the door lock and opened the door . . . only to find my mother passed out unconscious on the living-room floor. I called the ambulance to administer aid to her. Thank God the ambulance came just in time to take her to Martin Luther King Jr. Hospital.

The paramedics directed me to ride in the ambulance next to my mother as they pushed the stretcher into the rear of the ambulance. I was a very young nervous wreck, with tears running down my face, saliva coming from my mouth, snot seeping from my nose.

I couldn't take my eyes off my mother while one of the men, dressed in his white outfit, carefully and repeatedly pushed down on her chest with both hands, trying to get a steady heartbeat and an accompanying breathing pattern.

They placed this clear breathing mask over her nose and mouth with one long clear tube connecting the mask to a huge oxygen tank. Her respirations were shallow and labored. When we arrived at the hospital, I waited in the waiting room for over four hours until Dr. Lloyd Armstead, sporting a Jheri curl and glasses, informed me that Momma was diagnosed with stage four lung cancer. He assured me that she was in good care at the hospital. My mother had quit smoking years ago, so we were surprised at the diagnosis.

Afterwards, my mother had to receive chemotherapy on a weekly basis. After the incident, Momma developed a very depressed personality from time to time. I knew she was a strong fighter, but at the same time, it seemed as though she was decaying as the chemo was eating away at her white blood cells. All of a sudden, my father began to call my mother quite frequently; then he started to show up often during his work hours and after he got off work as well. He would stay for hours. Something in me would sometimes entertain the thought of my parents getting back together. But I would never put too much into that thought because I'd never really known that life. I think it was too late to fill that void Momma had in her heart for him.

My father came around more and more, driving his white Buick Electra 225. I am not sure the year of the car.

My mother would often mention to me how much she missed my daddy throughout the years. It seemed as if she spent the rest of her life raising me and trying to replace him. On October 30 of that year, 1985, nine months after the diagnosis, my mother lost her battle with cancer, which left me with a great deal of emotional wounds. I was only twenty years old at the time.

Although the cancer got the best of my mother, I felt she did the best she could do in raising a young black boy. She provided the best love and care a mother could. I'd always been proud of my mother. She never did anything that made me feel ashamed, such as have boyfriends in and out the house at night. Although she passed away from the cancer, I think her broken heart played a big part of her illness as well. Her death left me despondent and dejected while I wept uncontrollably for days.

My father arranged and paid for my mother's funeral. It was held at my mother's church, Saint Rest Baptist. The church was filled with beautiful flowers: carnations and roses. The smell of the roses reminded me of her perfume I used to slap on when I went to my junior high school dances. The Reverend Dr. William Hill performed the eulogy with what seemed like the whole neighborhood of Watts in attendance. The funeral procession snaked through Watts with over a hundred cars driving onto the Lincoln Cemetery in Compton on November 4.

And just like at my uncle Sonny Boy's funeral, the people cried, laughed, joked, and cried some more, as we all sat around the house reminiscing in sorrow.

Hours after my mother's funeral, I had an idea to get high, to help me get through the hurt and pain, to ease the burden of losing my mother. I shared my idea with Charlie. He suggested that we try the new alcohol that was out at that time. In my neighborhood, there would always be these large billboards advertising the newest brand of liquor to try, as if we were guinea pigs. I guess they were right because we got some of that liquor, and we also thought we'd try sniffing glue as well to get high; I couldn't remember whose idea that was.

So we went to the liquor store on 109th and Wilmington and waited outside to catch someone that would do us a favor by going into the store and buying the liquor for us. We were lucky to find a guy of age to buy the liquor, but we had to give him an extra dollar for the favor.

Charlie had the glue at home, already from the plastic model cars we used to build together. We put the glue in a plastic bag and held the bag over our mouths as we breathed in and out in order to inhale the vapor from the glue to give us a contact high. Man, that was a very bad idea.

At first, it was fun, but when we got high, we couldn't handle it. We were so intoxicated in an egregious way. We consumed too much liquor for our very first time drinking, and we absolutely did not know what we were actually during to ourselves, we were so engrossed in getting high. My head was spinning. I started to feel nauseated, and I then proceeded to vomit everywhere. I began to pray, "God, O God, if you pull me through this, I will never do it again."

Meanwhile, Charlie was drunk to the extent when he needed to pee, he staggered and stumbled over to the alley as he could barely walk, and just stood there, but he forgot to pull out his pecker, so he stood there and pissed on himself.

That was about the time the police pulled up and shined their light on us. They took us both to jail for public intoxication and underage drinking. Even though we were out of school, we weren't twenty-one yet. That's when I had to make that one and only phone call they give you in jail. I had to really make this call count because my mother was no longer there to come and get us out like she did when we were younger. So I called my father. He came down to the jail and bailed us out.

My father and I formed a bond ever since that day. I eventually moved in with him over in Inglewood. I didn't know my father had gotten a divorce about two years prior. I guess the recurrent visits he paid to me and my mother years ago when my mother was sick were the prelude into the transition of single parenting for my parents, because I still needed some growing up to do. Living with my father was interesting, although I was a young adult. He had a benevolent dictator personality, but I also recognized a lot of me in his ways. My father was a meek and mild man, and he enjoyed drinking gin and tonic. He gave me the guest room, and I took the initiative to do the cooking and cleaning that Momma taught me. My father loved the collard greens I would cook, along with the meat loaf my mother showed me how to prepare.

Sometimes it would seem as if he were trying to make up for old times or trying to catch up with time lost. I didn't hold any grudges against him for not being around much during my early youth because just living life with my mother was what I had grown to know, and I was content with that.

As a young adult in the big city, there were still some things I knew I could use my father's help with. Because I really didn't know which direction I needed to go as an adult, life got a little scary when I felt I didn't have anyone in my corner from time to time once my mother passed away. My father seemed as if he really wanted to be in my corner and help pull me through and see me succeed in life.

CHAPTER 12

The big test came when I was out of work when Zodys went out of business. My father let me live there with him without a job. We lived off his salary as our only income for about four months. I would be in and out of work without paying him a dime. I was thinking I really needed to find an occupation to make it in this society . . . until I was lying down in my bed one day and I got a call from one of my old junior high school buddies, Clifford. He said that he was calling looking for a rapper to start a real group to make some money. That's when I sat up in bed and my antennas shot up as I started to listen intensely to his plan and interject my own ideas. I suggested that we reach back to the junior high school days and look for Kenneth Potts to join us. Then Clifford told me that he had contacted Kenneth already, and he was down with the idea, and we would meet over at Clifford's house on 110th and Lou Dillon Street in Watts for rehearsals since we all were familiar with the location. Everybody knew his parents, Johnnie Mae and Benny; they were loved and well known around Watts. So we were able to spend many hours rehearsing all night.

The first thing we did was to establish our individual rap names. Clifford took on the rap name of "C-Note," because he was into music; Kenneth went with "K. P." due to his initials. I wanted to go with "Nate Dog" because of my first name being Nathaniel and many rappers were calling themselves dogs, but a rapper from Long Beach was already calling himself Nate Dogg, and I didn't want a rap beef too soon in my rap career, so I went with "Crazy Nate." That's what Kenneth was calling me back when I followed him into the bathroom back in junior high school and wanted to fight him while he was using the bathroom. Therefore, Crazy Nate was my rap name.

Now we had to come up with a name for our group. We threw around many names. Then I came up the name "The No Tones," due to all of the R&B groups and rappers who were joining in together making their songs, singing and rapping together. We wanted to pull away from R&B trying to be from the streets. Therefore, The No Tones was the name of our group, and then we decided to use the acronym of TNT.

We were on our way to stardom as we started with the raps that I wrote back in the day. Then they were suggesting that I let them write their own rhymes that would fit each one of their personalities, because there was no way possible we were alike as rappers. Clifford

"C-Note" was more of a smooth, laid-back rapper, directing his raps toward the ladies something like what Charlie would do, more so to get in the girls' pants.

Kenneth "K. P." was more on the gangster side of rapping, about driving by other gangsters in his car and shooting at them with his .9-mm pistol and .12-gauge shotgun out of his car window, robbing people, and selling drugs, and all the stuff he heard the RAS gang was doing in Watts back in the day when we were growing up. He would always use the phrase "My nigga" instead of addressing dudes by their name. He was also the first dude I heard use the term with other people. The first time he called me his "nigga," we had a big dispute. He claimed that it was a term of endearment; nevertheless, when we would disagree with anger, the first verbal weapon he would use against me was the word "nigga"! Delivered with just the right amount of anguish.

Now I, "Crazy Nate," on the other hand, was more of the conscience rapper, rapping about black pride and self-worth. I got more of my rapping and thinking from what I was hearing back in the day from the Black Panthers, Malcolm X, and Martin Luther King.

We had an awesome connection, and we would give the people a little of everything when we performed. So we would spend our weekdays rehearsing in Watts with the instrumental B-sides of the rap albums of the Sugarhill Gang, and Run-DMC because we didn't have a deejay as a rap group. Then we would pile into my car on the weekends to hit the local clubs around Los Angeles. The first club we hit was the Eve After Dark on Avalon and El Segundo on a Friday night; the club was packed. We arrived at the club seeking a rap battle in which we could battle and complete against other rap groups to show our rap skills; however, the Eve After Dark was not a hip-hop club, and the club had a strict dress code in order to ensure a certain type of crowd. The bouncer at the door wouldn't let us in wearing our hip-hop attire with Adidas sneakers and baggy jeans.

There weren't many hip-hop clubs around Los Angeles in those days; however, this one club near the Los Angeles Airport by the name of the Carolina West would put on hip-hop competitions. On these hip-hop nights, the club attire was strictly hip-hop wear, and the music was all rap. We had some real strong opponents, but the harder they came, the harder they fell. We won the contest that night, along with the thousand dollars cash prize, which also put us on the top of the list of the local circuit.

We split the money between the three of us. I took my money and went straight home to share it with my father for the bills that I was creating with food and utilities. One of the main things my father taught me while living with him was to take care of your bills where you lay your head before doing anything else with your money. My father saw that I was trying to become a responsible adult with my money and struggling at the same time. Therefore, he wouldn't accept all my money; just what it took to pay the utilities. The reminder of my money went into my car, as I would always have to repair something on it. My clothes were simple with jeans, T-shirts, and Adidas sneakers.

We kept on rehearsing, and I continued writing some of our rap songs. We kept searching for rap competitions to win money until we heard about a hip-hop competition that was being held in Hollywood on Hollywood Boulevard at the Florentine Gardens nightclub. The club advertised an enormous prize of $10,000 for the winner, $1,000 for the second place, and so on—but there was a catch: in order to get in the contest, there was a high entry fee of $30 to $50. If you were an artist, then it was $30; if you were a group, then it was $50, but we didn't read the fine print.

We discovered that the competition sponsors and the club owner reserved the right to award prizes on a prorated basis. The number of groups or artists that entered the contest so they could profit, no matter what, determined the real amount.

When we entered the contest, I had to take a loan from my father due to the money I had to pour into my car every other week. I didn't have a cent to my name, and since it didn't rain much in California, I didn't see a need to save for a rainy day.

When I drove over to Watts to pick up C-Note and K. P. to go the club, I was all hyped up to win the money. When I arrived, K. P. was drinking some Old English 800 malt liquor beer, and he was feeling a little drunk. Then he started making a big fuss about writing his own rap songs and trying to get C-Note to agree that we all write our own raps. At first, I took offense to the idea, then I agreed to let them do their own writing—after we entered the competition that evening.

When we were traveling from Watts to Hollywood, we were imagining and entertaining the thought of maybe using the contest as a springboard for a rap contract with a major record company like Def Jam or Ruthless Records. We started rapping on our way to the club in freestyle. We arrived at the club, and the line was around the Hollywood block with a variety of nationalities amongst the partygoers. We stood in the line and paid $20 each to get into the club, and we had to pay $50 on behalf of the TNT group to get in the competition.

We signed up for the competition, and as we were waiting for the contest to start, we moved around the club to mingle with the fly girls. We separated and started partying in different parts of the club. I proceeded to the back of the club following a nice young fly girl that I wanted to get to know, and once I caught up with her, I cleared my throat and began to make my approach—right when C-Note tapped me on the shoulder to inform me that K. P. was over at the bar drinking excessively. We did a U-turn toward the bar—to find K. P. too impaired to articulate words, let alone try to rap on stage. As the contest was starting, C-Note and I knew we had a problem on our hands if we were going to try to win the contest. We tried to enter the contest without K. P., but once again, we did not read the fine print stating that once you entered the contest, there could be no changes made and absolutely no refunds. So we still had to go in as a three-man group.

We were the fourth group to perform, and as we waited to go up, I began to argue with K. P. while C-Note was trying to sober him up by feeding him coffee and water. As the third act was ending their set, K. P. was assuring us that he was up to performing on stage, so we took his word and prepared to take the stage. Once the group finished their act, we stormed the stage full of hype. We had the whole club crowd with their hands in the air, waving them from side to side, as they bounced to the instrumental of Run-DMC's song "Rock Box." C-Note kicked off the song with his verse, and then as soon as I was about to say my verse, K. P. cut in and started saying verses that I didn't write and that didn't fit the music we rehearsed for—they were out of place. Then he began to step in front facing me, indicating he was trying to battle me. The crowd stopped waving their hands in the air and began to place their hands over their mouths, and then begin to boo us off the stage. It was obvious that we lost the competition and embarrassed ourselves. I went home broke and upset. As we left the club, the first thing that came to my mind was to kick K. P. out of the group.

We drove home from Hollywood back to Watts with the tension in the car growing into heavy silence. The silence was soon broken due to a loud noise that came from beneath the hood of my car, which forced me to pull over and investigate what sounded like damage to the engine. The first thought that occurred to me was to call my father to help us evaluate the problem. Between the three of us, I was the only one with some auto mechanic knowledge, and that was minimal due to the few breakdowns I'd had with my first outdated used car.

My father drove over to the location where we were stranded between Hollywood and Watts, right in the middle of South Central Los Angeles, with the local tow truck company en route. He and the tow truck driver inspected my car's engine and determined the oil pump had just gone out, which explained the loud knocking noise in the engine.

Next, my father and I had to drive C-Note and K. P. home over in Watts. After taking my friends home, we met the tow truck driver over at our home in Inglewood. I was back to square one with no money and now no running car to go job hunting, so I found myself back on the RTD, traveling across town searching for a job to get my car fixed and to lighten the load for my father with the utility bills.

During my time catching the bus around town in search of some financial remuneration, I was making sure to keep the group together by calling K. P. and C-Note. We agreed to write our own raps and try to make some money to get this whole rap thing off the ground; we saw other rap groups coming out of Compton, Los Angeles, and Watts making it big in the business.

By now, we were six months knee-deep in the rap and hip-hop culture to where we felt we just had to be a part of it, just like when I used to see Smokey Robinson and the Miracles in Will Rogers Park at the Watts festivals. Hip-hop made me feel good, like when I used to perform for my mother and her friends in the living room. We had the fire in us to go to the top. We believed we were a phenomenon.

C-Note tracked down Smitty the dope-man from back in the day over in Hollywood to purchase a large quantity of weed to sell on the side while working at the carwash to make ends meet. He was able to buy a 1976 gray Vega to help the group get around when my car was down.

We were making our way through the city's smog, and it was growing thicker than ever. I was still on the bus, and time moved on as the RTD had changed the name of the company to the Metro Bus Company. We were working the small nightspots. Wherever we could get rap work, we were there.

Then Clifford was stopped and pulled over for not wearing his seat belt. His car was searched with the police K-9, and they discovered a kilo of weed stashed underneath the backseat. K. P. and I actually dodged a bullet, as C-Note was en route to pick us up to attend a hip-hop show. C-Note's car was impounded, and he was subsequently indicted for drug possession. K. P. and I spent the first two months trying to collect funds to bail him out, but our efforts were in vain. C-Note was sentenced to five years in Chino Penitentiary. We started off catching the Metro to go visit him until it became a burden on us, and we quit.

A few months passed, and K. P. and I were still struggling as a rap duo due to our personality clashes, which became problematic as I felt that he carried around a huge bravado personality. It became apparent that the group was in danger of breaking up. Therefore, I was back to riding the Metro around town trying to find work. A chain of events began to occur when K. P. dropped by my house one day with a carload of gangsters to announce that he was quitting the TNT group to join the gangster rap group from Compton named Gangster Crew. He felt that the black conscience raps that I was writing, and the things I was rapping about, had played out, and gangster rap was the hottest music coming around. So therefore, I had become an anomaly in the rap game.

I realized that the rap music was changing, and I needed to make some money to help my father and get my car fixed. I didn't ever want to end up doing a crime to get by, and I didn't want to go in the direction of my old rap group counterparts, so it was quite evident that I needed to focus on getting a job and trying to do something with my life before my father became fed up with me living off of him. The thought of serving my country had crossed my mind several times, as I had not prepared myself for life once I left high school. Joining the armed forces wasn't too common among my peers in those days

When Ronald Reagan was leading the country, it seemed as if his whole political agenda showed disregard for people like me. Therefore, the desire to put my life on the line for what he represented at the time didn't make my kind feel too proud. Although the propaganda that he was selling was tempting, "Be All You Can Be," I knew I had to make a move and do it soon. I went down to the recruiting office to take the test for the army just to get a clear understanding on just what Uncle Sam wanted me for. All I knew was what I saw on those posters with an image of an Uncle Sam pointing his finger straight at me with the bold writing: UNCLE SAM WANTS YOU!

I went in, took the test, and passed with a high score. The recruiter asked me when I would like to leave for boot camp. At that point, I got really nervous. I had to think about it, so I made up an excuse to leave and told him that I'd be back the next day with an answer. I left the office to continue my job search.

CHAPTER 13

I made it home later that day, and I just knew I had to get a plan together because, lo and behold, I received a phone call from Linda on a Sunday night. When it rains, it pours. Linda told me that something was on her mind, and she felt that she had to tell me. At that point, I got very silent on the phone.

She said, "Well, I need to let you know that I am seven months pregnant with your baby."

"Why did you wait seven months to contact me about this issue?"

"Because I didn't quite believe that the baby belonged to my new boyfriend."

"I don't believe a goddamn thing that you have to say," I said. "And what about that big buff dude you cheated on me with? What about *him?*" I was still nursing my wounds that had been left unattended for far too long. I never did get the chance to curse her ass out for cheating on me. All that anger came back to revisit my broken heart, which had just begun to mend. "I need a paternity test to prove the things you are telling me," I said nastily. Ha! That would show her! I had no trust in her.

"So meet me over at the Watts Health Foundation Clinic when the baby is born, and we can take a paternity test," she offered.

I agreed. In the meantime, I needed to have a serious talk with my father about this situation I had gotten myself into. Although I enjoyed rolling around in the sack with Linda, I sure now regretted not using protection on my pecker.

My father expressed how serious this matter would be if the child was mine. He also expressed that a child must have both parents in its life. He hinted about how he struggled with his actions when he left my mother and me back in the day. He subsequently entered into a long lecture about young black children born out of wedlock and how essential it is for a father to be in the child's life. I was looking at my father and saying to myself, *This guy must be trying to atone for his past.*

I managed to fall asleep near the end of my father's lecture. The next morning, I woke up, and I had this whole baby thing heavy on my mind. During those two months of waiting for the baby to be born, Linda would call me and threaten me with having to pay child support. I was shitting bullets because I knew I didn't have a pot to piss in or a window to throw it out of. In the meantime, I had to file for some financial assistance.

I caught the Metro over to the unemployment office on 108th and Central. It was just down the street from where my uncle Sonny Boy was killed. The woman behind the desk helped me fill out the paperwork in order to get some kind of financial help to give my father so I could help with the bills and give Linda some money to help in preparation for the baby.

When I left the unemployment office, I thought to myself that it seemed like a recurrent cycle with men in my family not being in the household with their children. I was just barely twenty years old at this time, and I was thinking how I could have gotten my first real girlfriend pregnant. I could hear my mother's voice telling me about my actions leading up to this consequence.

Meanwhile, I felt I had to hit the yellow pages and the streets in pursuit of work. I looked for work here, there, and everywhere. My father would help to keep me prayed up like my mother told me when she gave me the little red Bible. He reminded me to stay positive. He would always tell me to keep my head up. "Don't worry because there is only one true Judge." Speaking of God, he would invite me to go to church with him; then he went out and bought me a big Bible, the kind with the gold-trimmed edges on fine, thin pages. He taught me how to navigate through the Bible in order to find the scripture I needed to help push and pull me through situations.

I also realized that all those times my mother would get on me about traveling alone, I wasn't ever really alone because God was always with me.

My father loved sharing Proverbs 2:2 about making your ear attentive to wisdom and inclining your heart to understanding. He also shared Proverbs 22:6 about training up a child in the way he should go; even when he is old, he will not depart from it.

Two months had passed, and I received a call from Linda two weeks after the birth, to announce the birth of the new baby boy she claimed was hers and mine. She had named him Robert after her then boyfriend. She wanted to confirm our meet time at the clinic for the paternity test. When she called, she told me that since I was the one that wanted the proof of the baby being mine, I would have to pay for the test. So I had to ask my father for a small loan until I got a job to pay him back.

When I got to the facility, I didn't even recognize Linda due to the weight gain, and although I was scared about the outcome, I was still anxious to see the baby and any resemblance to me, if there was any. The baby was a handsome little fellow, but I didn't see any resemblance between him and me. I looked at the baby and glared up at Linda and just said, "Okay, let's do this." We met with Doctor Melody Smith, one of the most serious doctors I've ever met in the waiting room, and she took us into the visiting room. She called it a noninvasive test; all she needed from the potential father was to take a swab from the inside of my mouth with a Q-tip. Then she conducted the procedure with the baby as well.

I went through the procedures, and Dr. Melody instructed us to wait seven days for the results. As we were leaving the clinic, Linda and I got embroiled in a verbal altercation about her cheating on me. I could not leave well enough alone. Linda had the nerve to tell me that I had been pushing her love in a different direction than she wanted, and that was the reason why she cheated on me, but nothing she could have said would have made me forgive her.

On that following Sunday, which was also seven days later, I went to the mailbox to see if my unemployment check arrived within the week. I open the mailbox and saw a letter with my name on it from the Watts Health Foundation that read in big bold letters CONFIDENTIAL. I opened the letter and read it. It said: *"We here at the Watts Health Foundation on behalf of Dr. Melody Smith regret to inform you that you have been excluded from the possibility of the paternity responsibility in which was brought and performed on behalf of Linda Baker."*

A wired feeling resonated through me with the relief of not being a young unwedded father; it was a load of responsibility lifted off my shoulders. I couldn't wait to call Linda and tell her about the letter, but when I called her, she was never available, so I stop calling. When I shared the news with my father, instead of one of his long lectures, he just simply said, "Son, you just dodged a bullet."

Just after Linda and the baby episode, I started to receive some good news when my unemployment checks started to come in. I began to keep some money in my pockets with my father showing me how to manage the little money that I did have.

There were times when the checks wouldn't come, and I was barely getting by. As a young adult, I would try to keep up with the Joneses and spend money I didn't have. Like one of the many times my car broke down, and I wanted to take Vanessa Miles on a date. We had to go to the drive-in on a double date. We went to the Vermont drive-in, and it was fun, but I could never get anywhere with Vanessa, because we were in the backseat of a friend's car, and we had no privacy.

I never liked asking my father for money because I didn't want him to think I was a burden. But, boy, I was catching the blues being so broke. I guess I had my pride. My father was always letting me know, in a sly way, that a man must go out and find work. He didn't have to tell me too many times because I didn't want to be thrown out. I noticed that Vanessa had stopped calling as well. I guessed it had something to do with me being broke.

CHAPTER 14

The city of Los Angeles was running on Olympic fever after just hosting the Olympic Games a few years earlier. The city was having their largest first-time City Marathon. The mayor and many other city leaders were scrambling to sweep the city clean—free from crime, drugs, and the homeless—in order to welcome the top-notch delegates that were visiting parts of the city. I wasn't interested in all the excitement that was going on due to the urgency about lining my pockets with some income.

One day when I was out job hunting, I bumped into my old buddy, Charlie. We were laughing and joking about the things we used to do back in the day and how we both had changed in appearance. Moments after all the laughter stopped, Charlie changed the conversation to tell me about his brother Big Rufus, who, unfortunately, met his demise when he was shot several times by a rival gang member while standing on the corner of Manchester and Denker. At the time, Big Rufus had given up the gang activities with the RAS gang, but he got hooked on crack cocaine, or crack rock, as some people called it. It was the drug that took the place of LSD (acid) in the eighties and nineties, and it wreaked havoc on the city along with the gangbangers.

Big Rufus had been hanging out on Manchester Boulevard, tripping out and acting weird when one of the up-and-coming young gangsters by the name of Little Stevie took notice of Big Rufus as an O. G (original gangster) from the RAS gang. Little Stevie was also the baby brother of one of the dudes that Big Rufus knocked out back in the day with one punch before the fight started. Therefore, the young gangster felt that if he killed Big Rufus, it would be payback for his big brother, along with earning some street credit among the gang members in his neighborhood.

Little Stevie walked right up to Big Rufus, acting as if he was an old admirer of the once-Watts Legend. He made his approach dressed in sagging Levi jeans, a white T-shirt, and brown Romeo shoe slippers. Then he stood there flexing his muscles like Big Rufus used to do back when he was younger. As soon as Big Rufus flashed a grin, Little Stevie smirked and pulled out his .9-mm pistol from his waistband, cocked back the hammer, and pointed it right at Big Rufus while squeezing the trigger, unloading the gun right then and there, shooting Big Rufus and hitting him in the head and chest in broad daylight.

During the police investigation, the cops noticed that there were video cameras mounted on the street signs—the whole incident was caught on surveillance camera. Little Stevie's face was plastered all over the television news channels and on America's Most Wanted. He was on the run for five days until he was tracked down and apprehended at his cousin Corky's house in Compton. Corky was a real solid dude; he used to study the Holy Qur'an, which is like the Bible, for the Islam religion. He convinced Little Stevie to turn himself in. Little Stevie was subsequently booked at the Compton sheriff's station on first-degree murder penal code 187. The young gangster was sentenced to life in prison without the possibility of parole. He was only sixteen years old, but the district attorney charged him as an adult, and he was sent to Folsom State Penitentiary.

Charlie also told me that he was enlisting in the army to straighten out his life, because he himself had gotten into a little trouble with the law. He revealed to me that he had gotten into the habit of stealing the radios out of expensive cars around Los Angeles. Then he would sell them to other folks in other cities.

He said that one day when he was pulled over by the cops for expired license plates on his car, they asked him if they could search his car. He said yes without thinking; and when they went to his trunk, he said he got sick in the stomach because he knew he was busted with the stolen radios in the trunk. They arrested him for stolen goods. He had to pay restitution to all of the victims and spend one year in the Los Angeles County Jail or enlist in the United States Army.

As Charlie and I wrapped up our conversation, I wished him well. He bid me good luck on my job hunting. While the job hunting was getting a little tougher, the city's demographics were slowly shifting; there was an influx of Latinos moving in and becoming your neighbor almost literally overnight. Some of the jobs were seeking Spanish-speaking or bilingual candidates only. Some of the native population found it a little difficult adjusting to one another until some kind of catastrophe or natural disaster affected the city, which would then bring almost all the citizens together. The large fires or earthquakes would frighten us all. Occasional unfair treatment by law enforcement of the new Latino population unable to fully understand the law, or against the black citizens considered a threat or a danger to the "natural order of things," according to the cops patrolling the streets, or with the mayor and the police chief turning a blind eye to the racial problems in the city—these negatives could sometimes bring unity among disparate people.

CHAPTER 15

Miraculously, the gangs in various parts of the city were talking about a gang truce after being tired of the gallons of blood being shed in the streets and spilling over into the sewage drains. The truce talk had Baptist ministers, Muslim ministers, Catholic priests, and other clergy galvanizing the gang members all over the city. Meetings were held at large hotels near LAX airport and in some backyards and churches.

The city had me feeling like I did when I was younger, when there was a sense of unity. Unfortunately, Big Rufus didn't live to see the day the gangs were coming together to call a truce. There was so much excitement pumping throughout the city. However, all the truce activities that were going on had the cops on high alert; they had never seen anything like the phenomenon that was occurring. Meetings took place in the neighborhood parks with different gang members welcoming their once rivals and enemies into their neighborhoods singing, dancing, and drinking beer by the forty ounces while celebrating a cease-fire.

During this time of celebration, I received a phone call from K. P. inviting me to attend a rap concert celebration as a solo act alongside his gangster rap group held at Will Rogers Park to acknowledge the partial gang truce. I thought to myself, this sounds good, and it would probably be like the Watts festivals that were held at the park many years ago. I was happy to be a part of the event. When the day came, I had to hitch a ride from my father to get to the park; he expressed his gratification about the endeavors of the local gangs. I felt butterflies in my stomach due to the anticipation of becoming a part of the city's history—the making of black history as far as I was concerned—because I'd seen firsthand how the gang activity had ruined the lives of many of our loved ones.

In essence, the whole-day event was leading to a peace treaty to end all street conflicts among all the gangs, with a performance by several rap groups and poetry reading, followed by community leaders' speeches, but not necessarily in that order.

I met up with K. P. and his crew on the corner of 103rd and Central Avenue. His group was dressed in black dickey suits and white All-Star tennis shoes and toting backpacks on their backs. I was dressed in contrast to K. P.'s crew with my brown button-down shirt, black baggy pleated slacks, and black patent leather pointed toe Stacy Adams shoes with my brown Kangol hat.

When I arrived at the park, the ambience had me feeling ecstatic and overjoyed. It was a peaceful scene like the one I'd seen in the park when I was a young child, minus the stony-faced stares from the cops. I was dominated by emotion when I noticed that the park had its name changed to Ted Watkins Park, the onetime old employer of my mother back in the day.

I was prepared to spit my conscience-focused, pro-black raps over a hip-hop instrumental, and I figured that was what the crowd wanted to hear instead of the gangster raps that K. P. and his backpack-toting crew was going to be spitting out. So I was kind of down for a small battle; rapping can be like a competitive sport. They looked soft by toting backpacks like little purses, and they were supposed to be gangster rappers.

Over three hundred gangsters and wannabe gangsters, followed with fly girls and gangster girls filled the park. The females were out and about dressed in Daisy Dukes and biker shorts with braids in their hair and doorknocker earrings in their ears. They were looking good and searching for the bad boys. City and community leaders attended, promoting themselves alongside demonstrations of community unity, hoping to be remembered when it came down to election time.

The religious leaders took the stage the first quarter of the day, addressing the crowd, passing the microphone over to the community leaders for the second quarter of the day, leaving the third quarter to the original gangsters. The last quarter of the day was the entertainment. I made it to the stage as the second to the last act, which was K. P. and his crew, as they thought that they would be last since their feelings were that no one could follow their rap act.

I got on stage and worked my magic on the crowd. A handful of the crowd wasn't feeling me, I could tell, with the folding of the arms and the vacant expressions on their faces. I continued to pump the crowd with my remixed version of "Fight the Power" by the rap group Public Enemy, then the crowd got hyped up. I looked over at K. P. and his crew, and they were mad-dogging me with envy. When I finished my set, I headed offstage toward K. P. and handed him the microphone while the crowd was cheering for more with their fists pumped in the air. When I handed him the microphone, he exchanged the mic for his backpack. Now he was on stage bouncing around with his crew, and I was being a spectator in the crowd holding a purse.

His gangster crew had the crowd rocking; their hands were in the air waving as if they just didn't care. They were performing a song by the rap group N.W.A. from Compton called "Gangsta, Gangsta." The crowd was extremely engaged as folks were dancing near the stage, which led to some rude behavior by two gangsters. Pushing and shoving was brought on by two more gangsters throwing up their gang signs using their fingers.

The performance stopped abruptly midway when gunfire erupted. Chaos consumed the entire park. People of all ages ran for cover, yelling and screaming and exiting the park in every direction. I began to run, slipping, sliding, and stumbling on the grass in my Stacy Adams and dropping my hat as I turned and looked back. I left it where it fell. I tried making my way to the streets while maneuvering toward 103rd Street. I sprinted for the Metro—only to be stopped by the cops, claiming I was running away with furtive movement by leaving my hat when it fell, which led to a search and seizure, which became a stop and detain based on reasonable suspicion, according the cops.

They suspected me of being armed and dangerous. A frisk for weapons made the stop reasonable as defined by the set of factual circumstances that led the cops to the park in the first place. Rightfully, they believed criminal activity was occurring as shots were fired. After stopping, they frisked me with a pat down. They detained me after they searched K. P.'s backpack that I was holding and discovered a .9-mm Beretta, along with a set of brass knuckles wrapped in a T-shirt.

I went from leaning on the front of the squad car with both hands spread out on the hot hood, to sitting in the backseat of the car, handcuffed, glaring out the window, feeling pissed off, puzzled, and petrified. Squad cars were racing to the park in every direction, apprehending anyone that they pleased present in a crime scene area. I guess in my case they felt lucky to have stopped me.

I was hauled off to the 108th Precinct, then booked and indicted on possession of a firearm. They granted me my one phone call to my father. He couldn't believe the charges; he was perplexed and bewildered. Then they placed me in a holding tank filled to capacity with a blend of petty thieves, drunks, muggers, and murderers waiting for a transport to various locations while being processed into the criminal justice system.

I was thrown in this intense, dangerous hellhole because I had been handed a backpack without knowing its contents. I felt like it was entrapment brought on by K. P., which had crossed my mind at the beginning of the process of my apprehension. However, I realized he couldn't have known someone would begin shooting while he was performing. The chaos that ensued left me literally "holding the bag." If only I had known the contents of the backpack, I wouldn't be sitting in this cage angrily trying to console myself with nowhere to place the blame.

As I sat in that cage, I was thinking about all the virtues my parents had tried to instill in me to avoid the situation I now found myself in. I could never have predicted this outcome. I cast aside my anger and allowed some fear to enter my thoughts. Where was my future headed now? The fear regarding my physical safety was in the back of my mind, especially when I thought about the prison stories Big Rufus would speak about on Hickory Street back in the day.

The officials took my mug shot, then I was fingerprinted. This was something I'd never looked forward to. I had seen some of the most notorious criminals enter the system, as well as some of the most innocent young black men who'd later been ushered into these same jail cells. My first two days I had a bad case of sleep deprivation and the gnawing uncertainty about the future.

On my third day in jail, a guard woke me up at 4:30 a.m., yelling my name with an early meal so that I could make it to my first court hearing. After I was given twenty minutes to eat my meal, I was escorted into the hallway with my right hand handcuffed to another guy's left hand as his right hand was cuffed to another guy's left hand. We were all linked and escorted out of the jail to an awaiting bus to take us to the courthouse in downtown Los Angeles. We remained handcuffed to each other all day unless someone had to use the restroom, but only if he had to have a bowel movement.

Once we all were in court, our names were read as we all lined up in front of the judge. The judge read the charges and penalties and explained them to each one of us, one at a time. When the judge got to me, he told me that I was charged with possession of a firearm and a felony charge of willfully discharging a firearm in a grossly negligent manner that could result in the death or injury to a person or persons, followed by a penalty of ten to fifteen years in state prison if convicted.

He also advised me of my rights to a speedy trial, and the right to a trial by jury, if I so desired. He then told me that I had the right to legal representation. I wasn't sure what that meant, and just when I was about to speak, he explained that the court can appoint a lawyer if I was too poor to afford a private lawyer.

At that moment, I asked the judge for one of those free lawyers that the court would give me. Right then, a short Chinese man wearing a suit two sizes too big for him walked over to me and told me to plead not guilty when the judge asked me how I pleaded. So when the judge asked, I yelled out, "Not guilty!" I felt that someone in this system was on my side to support me. The gentleman never told me his name at the time, but only that he would speak with me soon when he came to visit the jail. I was sent back to jail after the judge heard my plea.

A day later, the Chinese lawyer came to visit me in jail like he said he would. This time, he introduced himself as Mr. Woo, a public defender assigned by the court. We spoke about the day the police stopped me and the event that had taken place in the park. I told him that it was an event to bring the gangs together to stop the killings. I wasn't sure if he believed my story about the backpack, but he said something in a duplicitous manner that made me feel a little uncertain about him. Before he left, he told me "guys who deal in violence attract violence."

The first two weeks of jail were the most difficult. I had to acclimate to jail life, so I had to learn how to deal with the rules and regulations from the guards and the inmates. I realized the system was designed to keep a person uncomfortable constantly. The jail was a cesspool of extortionists, gangsters, and rapists of all kinds; therefore, confrontation became a part of my day in that hostile environment. One dude thought I was becoming a little vulnerable when he approached me, I guess due to the depression that I was starting to display as I became lost in deep thinking. I knew that I had to set the record straight with this guy because I might have to deal with him again. The physical altercation started with me squaring off with him, not really knowing what his beef and intention were; however, he approached me with aggression and mischief. I hit his ass with a flurry of punches as he stepped back, twisting his ankle and falling to the ground, yelling and screaming for the guards who struck me across the back with a nightstick while they pulled me off his ass. Then they dragged me out into another cell.

I knew I had grown up seeing and hearing about a lot of violence, but I never took part in any of it. I did want to become an enigma, but something inside of me told me that I better adapt to the way of life in this jail and defend myself to the best of my ability. My humanity began to shift into a warrior stance because it was about survival of the fittest. So while I was placed in a cell by myself, I worked on my mental and physical strength as my conscience spoke, telling me how I viewed myself had little to do with how those other guys viewed me, and that it was important for me to stand my guard. Every day, I would make sure I ate my meals and did my calisthenics workouts. Eating was important because when I was depressed early in my incarceration, I found myself missing meals and becoming increasingly weak, and jail is no place for a weak person, mentally or physically. There were numerous stories circulating around the jail about many of the young guys committing suicide or just going crazy due to their incarceration.

In no way did I feel that I owed a debt to society. This was a pivotal time in my life: I could either fight or fold. I thought of my mother, father, and the strength of God—all of which allowed me to fight to push and pull me through that bondage I found myself in.

After two and a half months in jail, I saw a stupendous rate of incarceration of young men. They came and went as the keys jingled and the barred doors slammed open and shut, guards yelling out booking numbers, and on and on. It was an endless rotation.

Early one morning as I slept, I was awakened by a guard yelling my name, telling me that I had visitors. I had to stand up, go over to the barred door, and extend both of my arms out of the open slot that the guards use to shove the meal plates through in order for him to place the handcuffs on me. Then he opened the door to place my ankles in shackles to escort me to the visiting room. The guard directed me to sit in booth number six. Once I sat down, I saw my father and another man dressed in a dapper suit. My father introduced the man to me as my lawyer, an associate partner of the Cochran law firm, by the name of Makenzine C. Johnson, attorney at law. The law firm had a well-earned reputation for tireless and effective legal representation, which was founded by the late Johnnie L. Cochran Jr., an excellent lawyer.

My father informed me that he put up his house for sale to retain Attorney Johnson to fight my case. I felt this was a heroic act on my father's part. My father assured me that everything would turn out just fine once Attorney Johnson got to work on my behalf. He was a very proud man, a meticulous dresser; he was also meticulous about how he spoke. He rarely misspoke, either, perhaps because he was very conscious that he was a role model and a professional.

Just after the visit, my father demanded that I not give up on myself. He was dedicated to pushing me through this difficult situation, and by the end of that day, I was out of jail on bail and waiting for my next court date to see if I would have to stand trial. I praised my father for getting me out of jail and after telling my story to Attorney Johnson. I was feeling good about the legal support he had provided for me. I knew Attorney Johnson was ready to fight my case.

I spent my idle time working on my car, tuning it up and changing the tires. I also tried to contact K. P. to see if he could help me out of this legal situation, but he was nowhere to be found, and that's the way he wanted it. I understood, to a certain extent, why he was avoiding me. To help me, he would probably have had to turn himself in.

My court date was Monday morning, and I had to be ready for anything. My father and I attended church that Sunday before court, and my father stood up in church to ask the congregation to pray that God and justice would see his son through the predicament he found himself in.

When we came home from church, my father and I enjoyed pizza and ice cream while watching sports all night together until it was time for me to go sleep. But I had no luck. I really could not sleep from thinking about the possible outcome of the hearing the next day.

My father came to my bedroom the next morning with a plate of eggs, sunny-side up, hash browns, bacon, and grits with a side of orange juice. I felt like it was my last meal. But my father was making the whole situation feel a little smoother as he drove me to the courthouse to meet up with Attorney Johnson.

Attorney Johnson assured me that he was going to take care of everything according to the research and work he had already done. He was confident that justice would prevail.

As we entered the courtroom, my father and I took a seat in the back of the courtroom, while Attorney Johnson spoke with the female clerk. Then he handed some papers over to her and had a seat on the defendant's side of the courtroom.

The bailiff spoke out and said, "All rise!" The entire room stood up, and the judge walked in and took a seat behind his large desk. The clerk called my name first, and Attorney Johnson waved his hand for me to come up. I stood next to him on the defendant's side with my right hand up to swear to tell the truth, the whole truth, and nothing but the truth, so help me God.

Then Attorney Johnson took over by speaking to the judge while the prosecutor listened in on the facts. I stood there watching solemnly, waiting on the outcome. He explained, displayed the evidence, and in layman's terminology, he told the court that my case was illogical because there was no way that I could have owned that gun and fired it in the park that day during the peace treaty. My fingerprints were nowhere on the gun, and the ballistics test showed that the gun had never been fired that day.

After Attorney Johnson presented his case, he motioned for the court to dismiss the charges against me and throw out the case. The judge looked over at the prosecutor, and my attorney said, "Move for dismissal." The prosecutor agreed just as the judge hit the gavel. I could just hear God speaking to me as he had done so many times in the past.

Attorney Johnson turned to me and shook my hand with a big smile as my father ran up to us both and hugged and squeezed me tightly and shook Attorney Johnson's hand as well. We all drove over to the nearest pizza parlor for pizza and ice cream.

CHAPTER 16

I tried to get my life back on track after serving almost six months in jail, and now searching for employment and realizing I owed a huge debt to my father. I told Dad about Charlie's story while we were both working on my car. My father was showing me how to replace the starter and change the oil. We both had all this gritty, black, sticky oil all over our hands. He then looked up at me and suggested that I enroll into Los Angeles Trade Technical College for Auto Mechanics. During that time, the auto mechanics trade was as popular as computer technicians are today. I took his suggestion and enrolled in the school. As I was attending school to study the trade, my father carried my load until I picked up a job at the Los Angeles Airport cleaning airplanes at night. I finally got my degree as an automotive mechanic, and I started working for Tune-up Masters, an auto repair chain on Florence and Main Street in South Central Los Angeles.

I was able to help my father out a lot more as his health had started to fail him. Dad was also a diabetic, and he would sometimes counsel me about death as if he was trying to prepare me for his death when he would experience complications with his diabetes. Once, while giving himself an insulin shot with a syringe, he taught me how to administer the shot so I could do it in case he couldn't.

Time seemed to zoom by, and even the weather changed with time. I had never experience snow in the city, but the city was caught up in a storm controlled by an abominable, diabolical snowman. This white stuff, however, wasn't snow at all. It was cocaine, and it was hitting the streets like a blizzard.

This cocaine storm was wiping out many black folks who couldn't say no, and who would not stop selling it. It was so cheap anyone could afford it once the dope dealer cooked the cocaine and turned it into crack rock. Black folks were beginning to lose their lives like pawns in a chess game. The chess game was being played with black folks' lives in the city. Many blacks also felt their culture was being replaced with the Latino culture, so it was also the season of black flight. Some blacks stayed in the city, and others who couldn't stand playing the game moved to the Inland Empire or the Valley, many miles away. Property values in the city dropped fast.

The game was in full-play mode. Drop-off houses were popping up everywhere around the city, replacing black folks with illegal, undocumented immigrants that were being transported to single-family homes and literally warehoused in garage spaces. The vast majority of the individuals transferred were family units with children from Central America and Mexico. The game was still being played with the new populations' lives. Meanwhile, the whole city demographic had changed completely, almost in an instant. I understood why Spanish wasn't taught in many of the so-called black school areas, and French was the second language: The schools were pushing this on us as a setup for the downfall when the influx of Latinos arrived by design. I think the change in population was all a part of the chess game plan, or what you would call *ethnic cleansing*.

Nevertheless, as time passed, urban Americans had to adjust in order to coexist. The city's racially disproportionate white police force was always met with fierce resistance as news channels would report images of police beatings and killings of undocumented citizens along with documented citizens, black and brown alike.

My father would give me long lectures on how to behave when the police approached or stopped me. Although I've had contact with the police back in the day when I was coming up, he felt that as the demographic changed throughout years, the police applied harsher tactics, some of which could lead to death. He told me to stay calm, not to resist physically, not to talk much, and know how to reach their captain in a hurry. He also said I should answer with "Yes sir" and "No sir" without sarcasm, because some of them would love to neutralize you. There were many young guys being killed by bad police gunfire, as if there was some kind of unspoken war declared, like it had been back in the day with the Black

Panthers. Some of the good cops would actually cover for the bad cops in the name of blue wall, similar to what the RAS Gang did in my old neighborhood.

I've never witness a killing, but one thing in life I knew was that death was certain. I thought back on my uncle Sonny Boy, my mother, and Big Rufus. It was now the nineties and the incidents of racial injustice and recurring police abuse of power against Blacks and Latinos living in Watts had not ceased. A powder keg was building.

One warm spring afternoon, sometime after March 3, 1991 my father and I were sitting back watching television, and the news flashed a breaking news report of a white police officer stopping and beating an unarmed black motorist. I couldn't believe my eyes and ears because the images clearly showed police brutality. The reporter named Officer Chad Austin of the Los Angeles Police Department as the cop involved. I knew I had remembered the officer's name from when I was in high school, and when they displayed his picture on the TV, I was sure that this was the same Chad Austin from Van Nuys High School, now part of this perverse system of law enforcement with his same old attitude. An oppressive inequality that demanded change had begun to hover over the city like never before.

From what I've heard about the year 1965, it seemed as though it was a case of déjà vu all over the city. After the verdict was announced a year later, on

April 29, 1992, a riot exploded. The fires spread over Los Angeles, Inglewood, Compton, and Watts, and then spilled over into Hollywood. This riot lasted for about two days.

Renegade cops were antagonizing the local folks, as the government allowed them to serve up ass whippings to the citizens in the name of "protecting the city structures." Opportunistic criminal actions by some of the residents were rampant, and a portion of the business owners was taking up arms against the looters. It seemed that imminent danger was everywhere.

At least thirty-six people died, and more than one thousand were injured. The city and businesses suffered billions of dollars in damage from arson and looting. Clergy leaders called for an end to the public disorder. The governor declared a state of emergency. The president of the United States called for law and order.

The police couldn't ensure the people due process of the law . . . because they themselves denied the people due process. Many of the people said: All we want is due process. However, the police that were in full combat mode ignored them. The National Guard was called in to enforce order and back the police. People were thrown in jail for long periods of time, and some were just missing in action. I felt like it was what I assumed war was like.

My father and I took shelter for three days as we shielded ourselves inside our home, in order to stay out of harm's way. My father led a prayer for the city as we kept glued to the media coverage on the television. While we were sheltered in our home, I questioned my father about his upbringing in this country as a black man with the injustice that was rampant during the Jim Crow era. He told me understanding the injustice had saved him from hatred. Where there is hatred, there is self-hate, and there's something very suicidal about that. He told me not to run away from the unknown and to seek information about something perplexing, because when you swim in ignorance, you end up frustrated, and your ignorance is empowering your oppressor. He also expressed his deepest regret for leaving my mother and I back in the day, knowing that the streets can do a very poor job in building black men, and it was important for me to see black men as positive role models.

After months passed with the city still smoldering with conflict and disarray, my father had to retire due to his health problems. The city instituted cutbacks, blaming it on city repairs due to the riot and the uprisings. Nevertheless, my father was steadfast on keeping me out of harm's way with all the tension on the streets throughout the cities of Southern California. Although I was a grown man, my father saw the world as a changing place and expressed his concern for my well-being. He also felt that the good and bad things happening in our city were a testament to the existence of a microcosm reflecting what was happening in other parts of our country.

He insisted that we spend quality time together, and I agreed because I didn't want to take the time we had together for granted, in part due to my reflecting back on the relationship I shared with my mother. He told me if I didn't use my time wisely, it could become my enemy, as time is arbitrary. We would get together and go over to the Hollywood Park racetrack to watch the horses run, and we loved sitting back with a cold beer watching boxing matches on TV.

As we got together to go to church, my father advised me to keep God first and hold on to my morals and my integrity, and if I did so, I would be okay.

I was finally on my feet with a steady job, taking care of my business like a man. I was still living with my father, and I didn't want to leave him home alone for too long. I guess you could say at that point in life, the roles were reversed. I loved caring for him every single day. Just like my mother, my father had become the most important person in my life next to God.

One day when I came home from work, my father and I had the idea to go out to a blues club on Avalon and 120th Street called The Lobby Inn. It was owned and run by twin brothers, Floyd and Lloyd. They gave my father and me complimentary treatment due to the fact they had known my father for many years.

My father had worn his gray and black tweed suit, a black shirt with a white *Godfather* hat, and black-and-white wingtip Stacy Adams shoes. Man, he was sharp as a tack. We had a good old time as we listened to Bobby "Blue" Bland, Johnnie Taylor, and some B. B. King all night until the club shut down.

We learned how to enjoy each other's company as father and son. I alternated my time between work, church, and being home with my father. I would date occasionally, but nothing serious.

My father kicked the gin and tonic drinking and became a full-fledged deacon at the same Saint Rest Baptist Church my mother and I used to attend many years ago, which was still under the leadership of Dr. Reverend William Hill.

My father had a hand in getting me to finally join the church and connect with the tenors in the choir. I really couldn't sing, but since I was in church, I didn't think anyone would kick me out of the choir. Besides, Charlie told me that the church was the place to find a good girl, the kind of girl my mother used to describe. I went to church every Sunday with my father. I looked for the good girls, but I was more interested in Reverend Hill's preaching.

CHAPTER 17

B y this time, the Los Angeles Raiders team had packed up and moved from Los Angeles back to Oakland, the Los Angeles commute improved with a new Metro Blue Line Train system, which was a leap from the old RTD bus I used to ride when I was much younger. Also, the eyes of the world focused on Los Angeles as football great O. J. Simpson was no longer running through airports and jumping over luggage; instead, he was running for his life in a slow-speed car chase. He was later arrested for the murder of his ex-wife. No longer was he America's hero. Eventually, he was found not guilty, contrary to some people's belief of what would have been a just verdict. The newly elected president Bill Clinton signed a bill into the three-strikes law, which significantly increased the prison sentencing of many people who had been previously convicted of two or more violent crimes or serious felonies. This law touched many black men, but this law did not discriminate.

As time passed on, two years later in October, my father's health took a turn for the worse, so I took him to see Dr. Melody Smith. Dr. Smith admitted him into Centinela Hospital in Inglewood. Just after being in the hospital for a day, he slipped into a diabetic coma. He stayed in the coma for two weeks while I camped out in his hospital room right beside his bed up until he succumbed to complications from diabetes on November 17, 2004.

I laid my father to rest on the twenty-sixth of November. I held his funeral at our church home, Saint Rest Baptist Church, and after the ceremony was held, once again, we all sat around sharing simultaneous laughter, tears, and jokes. Every once in a while, I would reminisce about my parents. I would put on a Bobby "Blue" Bland song called "Ain't No Love in the Heart of Town."

As it turned out, my father left his house and a sum of money in his last will and testament for me to open my own auto repair garage. I became an entrepreneur. I was happy because being a young entrepreneur, one was considered a good citizen in my city. I was baptized and became a deacon at the church. I began to help out more in the music department with writing some of the songs for the choir like I had done with the rap group many years before.

A year later, the church put on a musical for the Easter Sunday program. We invited a guest church to the musical, the Double Rock Baptist Church from Compton, to headline the program. It was an all-day delight. During the program, while I was sitting in the congregation with my head bowed, Pastor Hill called out to all the worshipers to come forward to signify their decision to commit their lives to God. The visiting choir started to sing a selection, and the woman leading the song began singing in an angelic voice, delivering a spiritual like angels rejoicing from up above.

I raised my head to catch a glance of this woman . . . and witnessed an astonishing moment in time. I was amazed to see it was Linda Baker from an old relationship belting out this glorifying song by Mahalia Jackson, "How I Got Over."

Tears filled my eyes as I stared at her throughout the entire selection. I was so moved to see Linda singing that song. When she ended the song, she smiled incandescently. Once the event was over, we both moved hastily toward each other and embraced. We both were happy to see each other as though our awful debacle many years ago had dissolved with the passage of time.

Now that I was seeing Linda in a more mature light, I had to recalibrate my expectations of her. Linda and I exchanged information and reached out to each other later in the week. We talked over the phone like we did when we were younger. Linda expressed how much she enjoyed singing and going to church and how difficult it was being a single mother. I asked her about support from the child's father, who was the same guy that she cheated on me with. She explained to me that there was nothing serious back then, and the relationship only lasted a month. The child's father was killed in the chaos of the last city riot, so he never played a role in the child's life. She had to raise the boy on her own.

The phone calls stayed consistent for about three months, which led to a small courtship, that erupted into a full-blown love affair. It's been those moments when I realized I was basically checking her out from a distance. She made me fall in love all over again. I would get this tinge of excitement when I remembered that this was the lady I was in love with. This was because her love and understanding went too deep to be damaged by a little distance and time. That is why being in love is so unbelievably incredible. My life feels like a string of happy and unhappy moments, and love is just composed of many of the happy ones.

I needed to meet her child who she called Little Robert. He was seven years old. Linda had done a wonderful job raising the young fellow to that point in his life, which wasn't too hard to understand because Linda had blossomed into a beautiful flower herself, so I thought that I had to pick her from the garden to be mine. I asked her to be my wife, and therefore, Little Robert became Little Robert Smith, taking on my last name, as did Linda. I was very sure about the decision, because I felt a strong love for the two of them, and I really understood the required sacrifices it was going to take in order to set Robert on the right track. I knew it was going to take the same kind of love my mother and father gave to me with the love of God, coupled with the knowledge of self-worth and the respect of others. It was a winning formula.

I really thanked God for placing Linda and Robert in my life to create a family union. Our union would bring about a good and positive change to the community and to the world as a whole. Parents bringing up a child in a loving household and keeping the child out of harm's way is the best thing, whether both parents are in his life or apart. Love for each other is always important because it maintains the connection with each other throughout the trials and tribulations of life.

We held the wedding at Saint Rest Baptist Church on July 2nd 2005 with Dr. Reverend William Hill doing the honors. My friend Charlie came home on leave to be my best man. Robert was the ring bearer. Linda managed to find her cousin Maxine clean and sober to be one of her bridesmaids. We were all dressed in hues of lavender and cream. It was a romantic, emotional ceremony. I was left feeling good as a breath of fresh air. It was also a little bittersweet because my parents weren't there to see that day, but I knew that they were there in spirit. I think one of the happiest things about the whole union was that Linda and I would be there to help push and pull Little Robert Smith through, so he would be able to fulfill God's purpose and plan for him in life.

Our happiness comes from the seeds we sow as the love we share continues to grow with passion and joy. Every day feels brand new all the way through, and we love to spend our Sundays after church driving west on Imperial Highway to Dockweiler Beach to watch the sunset.

One thing I know for sure is that with both my mother and my father gone from this earth, I will keep them in my heart. I understood my parents were praying people, which is something that was eventually instilled in me, and I believe prayer and faith in God will sustain me through the many obstacles and ills in this world. I'm truly glad to have had my parents introduce God into my life as he protects me. I'm grateful for every time he continues to help push and pull us through.

When Satan enters into our communities to attack us as the author of confusion, with many trials and tribulations, we counterattack with prayer and faith as our weapons, while the will of God is manifest in our hearts and minds *To Help Push and Pull Us Through.*

Dear God, please answer my call,
I need you to do all that you said
you would do.

Dear God, please take my hand.
It feels like I've taken all that I can stand.

When I stumble, fall, and
I know I've given it my all,
I look to you to answer my call.

I know this fight is not mine.
God, I need you on the main line.

God, I love you, and I know you love me too.
God, I'm calling on you to pull me through.

Dear God, please answer my call,
Dear God, please answer my call.

I know when I call on you
I should never have to worry,
But, God, I need you in a hurry.

Dear God, please answer my call,
please send me a sign, just to let me know
that I'll be next on your prayer line.

Dear God, I'll hold on, sit here, and wait, because
I know you have a lot on your plate.

Dear God, I'm calling on you,
To Help Push and Pull Me Through.

www.ingramcontent.com/pod-product-compliance
Lightning Source LLC
Chambersburg PA
CBHW051836040426
42447CB00006B/557